Harvard
Business
Review

ON

TURNAROUNDS

THE HARVARD BUSINESS REVIEW PAPERBACK SERIES

The series is designed to bring today's managers and professionals the fundamental information they need to stay competitive in a fast-moving world. From the preeminent thinkers whose work has defined an entire field to the rising stars who will redefine the way we think about business, here are the leading minds and landmark ideas that have established the *Harvard Business Review* as required reading for ambitious businesspeople in organizations around the globe.

Other books in the series:

Harvard Business Review Interviews with CEOs

Harvard Business Review on Brand Management

Harvard Business Review on Breakthrough Thinking

Harvard Business Review on Business and the Environment

Harvard Business Review on the Business Value of IT

Harvard Business Review on Change

Harvard Business Review on Corporate Governance

Harvard Business Review on Corporate Strategy

Harvard Business Review on Crisis Management

Harvard Business Review on Decision Making

Harvard Business Review on Effective Communication

Harvard Business Review on Entrepreneurship

Harvard Business Review on Finding and Keeping the Best People

Harvard Business Review on Innovation

Harvard Business Review on Knowledge Management

Harvard Business Review on Leadership

Harvard Business Review on Managing High-Tech Industries

Harvard Business Review on Managing People

Harvard Business Review on Managing Uncertainty

Harvard Business Review

ON

TURNAROUNDS

A HARVARD BUSINESS REVIEW PAPERBACK

The *Harvard Business Review* articles in this collection are available as
individual reprints. Discounts apply to quantity purchases. For information and ordering, please contact Customer Service, Harvard Business
School Publishing, Boston, MA 02163. Telephone: (617) 783-7500 or
(800) 988-0886, 8 A.M. to 6 P.M. Eastern Time, Monday through Friday.
Fax: (617) 783-7555, 24 hours a day. E-mail: custserv@hbsp.harvard.edu

Library of Congress Cataloging-in-Publication Data
Harvard business review on turnarounds.
     p. cm. — (A Harvard business review paperback)
    Includes bibliographical references and index.
    ISBN 1-57851-636-6 (alk. paper)
    1. Corporate turnarounds. I. Title: Turnarounds. II. Harvard
business review. III. Harvard business review series.
HD58.8 .H3696 2001
658.4′063—dc21   2001039413
                                                        CIP

*The paper used in this publication meets the requirements of the Ameri-
can National Standard for Permanence of Paper for Publications and
Documents in Libraries and Archives Z39.48-1992.*

Contents

Harvard Business Review

ON

TURNAROUNDS

Cracking the Code of Change

MICHAEL BEER AND NITIN NOHRIA

Executive Summary

TODAY'S FAST-PACED ECONOMY demands that businesses change or die. But few companies manage corporate transformations as well as they would like. The brutal fact is that about 70% of all change initiatives fail.

In this article, authors Michael Beer and Nitin Nohria describe two archetypes—or theories—of corporate transformation that may help executives crack the code of change. Theory E is change based on economic value: shareholder value is the only legitimate measure of success, and change often involves heavy use of economic incentives, layoffs, downsizing, and restructuring. Theory O is change based on organizational capability: the goal is to build and strengthen corporate culture.

Most companies focus purely on one theory or the other, or haphazardly use a mix of both, the authors say. Combining E and O is directionally correct, they contend, but it requires a careful, conscious integration plan. Beer and Nohria present the examples of two companies, Scott Paper and Champion International, that used a purely E or purely O strategy to create change—and met with limited levels of success.

They contrast those corporate transformations with that of UK-based retailer ASDA, which has successfully embraced the paradox between the opposing theories of change and integrated E and O. The lesson from ASDA? To thrive and adapt in the new economy, companies must make sure the E and O theories of business change are in sync at their own organizations.

The New Economy has ushered in great business opportunities—and great turmoil. Not since the Industrial Revolution have the stakes of dealing with change been so high. Most traditional organizations have accepted, in theory at least, that they must either change or die. And even Internet companies such as eBay, Amazon.com, and America Online recognize that they need to manage the changes associated with rapid entrepreneurial growth. Despite some individual successes, however, change remains difficult to pull off, and few companies manage the process as well as they would like. Most of their initiatives—installing new technology, downsizing, restructuring, or trying to change corporate culture—have had low success rates. The brutal fact is that about 70% of all change initiatives fail.

In our experience, the reason for most of those failures is that in their rush to change their organizations, managers end up immersing themselves in an alphabet soup of initiatives. They lose focus and become mesmerized by all the advice available in print and on-line about why companies should change, what they should try to accomplish, and how they should do it. This proliferation of recommendations often leads to muddle when change is attempted. The result is that most change efforts exert a heavy toll, both human and economic. To improve the odds of success, and to reduce the human carnage, it is imperative that executives understand the nature and process of corporate change much better. But even that is not enough. Leaders need to crack the code of change.

Theory E change strategies usually involve heavy use of economic incentives, drastic layoffs, downsizing, and restructuring. Shareholder value is the only legitimate measure of corporate success.

For more than 40 years now, we've been studying the nature of corporate change. And although every business's change initiative is unique, our research suggests there are two archetypes, or theories, of change. These archetypes are based on very different and often unconscious assumptions by senior executives—and the consultants and academics who advise them—about why and how changes should be made. Theory E is change based on economic value. Theory O is change based on organizational capability. Both are valid models; each theory of change achieves some of management's goals, either explicitly or implicitly. But each theory also has its costs—often unexpected ones.

Theory E change strategies are the ones that make all the headlines. In this "hard" approach to change, shareholder value is the only legitimate measure of corporate success. Change usually involves heavy use of economic incentives, drastic layoffs, downsizing, and restructuring. E change strategies are more common than O change strategies among companies in the United States, where financial markets push corporate boards for rapid turnarounds. For instance, when William A. Anders was brought in as CEO of General Dynamics in 1991, his goal was to maximize economic value—however painful the remedies might be. Over the next three years, Anders reduced the workforce by 71,000 people—44,000 through the divestiture of seven businesses and 27,000 through layoffs and attrition. Anders employed common E strategies.

Managers who subscribe to Theory O believe that if they were to focus exclusively on the price of their stock, they might harm their organizations. In this "soft" approach to change, the goal is to develop corporate culture and human capability through individual and organizational learning—the process of changing, obtaining feedback, reflecting, and making further changes.

Theory O change strategies are geared toward building up the corporate culture: employee behaviors, attitudes, capabilities, and commitment. The organization's ability to learn from its experiences is a legitimate yardstick of corporate success.

U.S. companies that adopt O strategies, as Hewlett-Packard did when its performance flagged in the 1980s, typically have strong, long-held, commitment-based psychological contracts with their employees.

Managers at these companies are likely to see the risks in breaking those contracts. Because they place a high value on employee commitment, Asian and European businesses are also more likely to adopt an O strategy to change.

Few companies subscribe to just one theory. Most companies we have studied have used a mix of both. But all too often, managers try to apply theories E and O in tandem without resolving the inherent tensions between them. This impulse to combine the strategies is directionally correct, but theories E and O are so different that it's hard to manage them simultaneously—employees distrust leaders who alternate between nurturing and cutthroat corporate behavior. Our research suggests, however, that there is a way to resolve the tension so that businesses can satisfy their shareholders while building viable institutions. Companies that effectively combine hard and soft approaches to change can reap big payoffs in profitability and productivity. Those companies are more likely to achieve a sustainable competitive advantage. They can also reduce the anxiety that grips whole societies in the face of corporate restructuring.

In this article, we will explore how one company successfully resolved the tensions between E and O strategies. But before we do that, we need to look at just how different the two theories are.

A Tale of Two Theories

To understand how sharply theories E and O differ, we can compare them along several key dimensions of corporate change: goals, leadership, focus, process, reward system, and use of consultants. (For a side-by-side comparison, see the exhibit "Comparing Theories of Change.") We'll look at two companies in similar businesses that adopted almost pure forms of each archetype. Scott Paper successfully used Theory E to enhance shareholder value, while Champion International used Theory O to achieve a complete cultural transformation that increased its productivity and employee commitment. But as we will soon observe, both paper producers also discovered the limitations of sticking with only one theory of change. Let's compare the two companies' initiatives.

Comparing Theories of Change

Our research has shown that all corporate transformations can be compared along the six dimensions shown here. The table outlines the differences between the E and O archetypes and illustrates what an integrated approach might look like.

Dimensions of Change	Theory E	Theory O	Theories E and O Combined
Goals	Maximize shareholder value	Develop organizational capabilities	Explicitly embrace the paradox between economic value and organizational capability
Leadership	Manage change from the top down	Encourage participation from the bottom up	Set direction from the top and engage the people below
Focus	Emphasize structure and systems	Build up corporate culture: employees' behavior and attitudes	Focus simultaneously on the hard (structures and systems) and the soft (corporate culture)
Process	Plan and establish programs	Experiment and evolve	Plan for spontaneity
Reward System	Motivate through financial incentives	Motivate through commitment—use pay as fair exchange	Use incentives to reinforce change but not to drive it
Use of Consultants	Consultants analyze problems and shape solutions	Consultants support management in shaping their own solutions	Consultants are expert resources who empower employees

GOALS

When Al Dunlap assumed leadership of Scott Paper in May 1994, he immediately fired 11,000 employees and sold off several businesses. His determination to restructure the beleaguered company was almost monomaniacal. As he said in one of his speeches: "Shareholders are the number one constituency. Show me an annual report that lists six or seven constituencies, and I'll show you a mismanaged company." From a shareholder's perspective, the results of Dunlap's actions were stunning. In just 20 months, he managed to triple shareholder returns as Scott Paper's market value rose from about $3 billion in 1994 to about $9 billion by the end of 1995. The financial community applauded his efforts and hailed Scott Paper's approach to change as a model for improving shareholder returns.

Champion's reform effort couldn't have been more different. CEO Andrew Sigler acknowledged that enhanced economic value was an appropriate target for management, but he believed that goal would be best achieved by transforming the behaviors of management, unions, and workers alike. In 1981, Sigler and other managers launched a long-term effort to restructure corporate culture around a new vision called the Champion Way, a set of values and principles designed to build up the competencies of the workforce. By improving the organization's capabilities in areas such as teamwork and communication, Sigler believed he could best increase employee productivity and thereby improve the bottom line.

LEADERSHIP

Leaders who subscribe to Theory E manage change the old-fashioned way: from the top down. They set goals with little involvement from their management teams and certainly without input from lower levels or unions. Dunlap was clearly the commander in chief at Scott Paper. The executives who survived his purges, for example, had to agree with his philosophy that shareholder value was now the company's primary objective. Nothing made clear Dunlap's leadership style better than the nickname he gloried in: "Chainsaw Al."

By contrast, participation (a Theory O trait) was the hallmark of change at Champion. Every effort was made to get all its employees emotionally committed to improving the company's performance. Teams drafted value statements, and even the industry's unions were brought into the dialogue. Employees were encouraged to identify and solve problems themselves. Change at Champion sprouted from the bottom up.

FOCUS

In E-type change, leaders typically focus immediately on streamlining the "hardware" of the organization—the structures and systems. These are the elements that can most easily be changed from the top down, yielding swift financial results. For instance, Dunlap quickly decided to outsource many of Scott Paper's corporate functions—benefits and payroll administration, almost all of its management information systems, some of its technology research, medical services, telemarketing, and security functions. An executive manager of a global merger explained the E rationale: "I have a [profit] goal of $176 million this year, and there's no time to involve others or develop organizational capability."

By contrast, Theory O's initial focus is on building up the "software" of an organization—the culture, behavior, and attitudes of employees. Throughout a decade of reforms, no employees were laid off at Champion. Rather, managers and employees were encouraged to collectively reexamine their work practices and behaviors with a goal of increasing productivity and quality. Managers were replaced if they did not conform to the new philosophy, but the overall firing freeze helped to create a culture of trust and commitment. Structural change followed once the culture changed. Indeed, by the mid-1990s, Champion had completely reorganized all its corporate functions. Once a hierarchical, functionally organized company, Champion adopted a matrix structure that empowered employee teams to focus more on customers.

PROCESS

Theory E is predicated on the view that no battle can be won without a clear, comprehensive, common plan of action that encourages internal coordination and inspires confidence among customers, suppliers, and investors. The plan lets leaders quickly motivate and mobilize their businesses; it compels them to take tough, decisive actions they presumably haven't taken in the past. The changes at Scott Paper unfolded like a military battle plan. Managers were instructed to achieve specific targets by specific dates. If they didn't adhere to Dunlap's tightly choreographed marching orders, they risked being fired.

Meanwhile, the changes at Champion were more evolutionary and emergent than planned and programmatic. When the company's decade-long reform began in 1981, there was no master blueprint. The idea was that innovative work processes, values, and culture changes in one plant would be adapted and used by other plants on their way through the corporate system. No single person, not even Sigler, was seen as the driver of change.

Instead, local leaders took responsibility. Top management simply encouraged experimentation from the ground up, spread new ideas to other workers, and transferred managers of innovative units to lagging ones.

REWARD SYSTEM

The rewards for managers in E-type change programs are primarily financial. Employee compensation, for example, is linked with financial incentives, mainly stock options. Dunlap's own compensation package—which ultimately netted him more than $100 million—was tightly linked to shareholders' interests. Proponents of this system argue that financial incentives guarantee that employees' interests match stockholders' interests. Financial rewards also help top executives feel compensated for a difficult job— one in which they are often reviled by their onetime colleagues and the larger community.

The O-style compensation systems at Champion reinforced the goals of culture change, but they didn't drive those goals. A skills-based pay system and a corporatewide gains-sharing plan were installed to draw union workers and management into a community of purpose. Financial incentives were used only as a supplement to those systems and not to push particular reforms. While Champion did offer a companywide bonus to achieve business goals in two separate years, this came late in the change process and played a minor role in actually fulfilling those goals.

USE OF CONSULTANTS

Theory E change strategies often rely heavily on external consultants. A SWAT team of Ivy League–educated

MBAs, armed with an arsenal of state-of-the-art ideas, is brought in to find new ways to look at the business and manage it. The consultants can help CEOs get a fix on urgent issues and priorities. They also offer much-needed political and psychological support for CEOs who are under fire from financial markets. At Scott Paper, Dunlap engaged consultants to identify many of the painful cost-savings initiatives that he subsequently implemented.

Theory O change programs rely far less on consultants. The handful of consultants who were introduced at Champion helped managers and workers make their own business analyses and craft their own solutions. And while the consultants had their own ideas, they did not recommend any corporate program, dictate any solutions, or whip anyone into line. They simply led a process of discovery and learning that was intended to change the corporate culture in a way that could not be foreseen at the outset.

Scott Paper's CEO trebled shareholder returns but failed to build the capabilities needed for sustained competitive advantage—commitment, coordination, communication, and creativity.

In their purest forms, both change theories clearly have their limitations. CEOs who must make difficult E-style choices understandably distance themselves from their employees to ease their own pain and guilt. Once removed from their people, these CEOs begin to see their employees as part of the problem. As time goes on, these leaders become less and less inclined to adopt O-style change strategies. They fail to invest in building the company's human resources, which inevitably hollows out the company and saps its capacity for sustained performance. At Scott Paper, for example, Dunlap trebled shareholder returns but failed to build the capabilities needed for sustained competitive advantage—commitment, coordination, communication, and creativity. In 1995, Dunlap sold Scott Paper to its longtime competitor Kimberly-Clark.

CEOs who embrace Theory O find that their loyalty and commitment to their employees can prevent them from making tough decisions. The temptation is to postpone the bitter medicine in the hopes that rising productivity will improve the business situation. But productivity gains aren't enough when fundamental structural change is required. That reality is underscored by today's global financial system, which makes corporate performance instantly transparent to large institutional shareholders whose fund managers are under enormous pressure to show good results. Consider Champion. By 1997, it had become one of the leaders in its industry based on most performance measures. Still, newly instated CEO Richard Olsen was forced to admit a tough reality: Champion shareholders had not seen a significant increase in the economic value of the company in more than a decade. Indeed, when Champion was sold recently to Finland-based UPM-Kymmene, it was acquired for a mere 1.5 times its original share value.

CEOs who embrace Theory O find that their loyalty and commitment to their employees can prevent them from making tough decisions.

Managing the Contradictions

Clearly, if the objective is to build a company that can adapt, survive, and prosper over the years, Theory E strategies must somehow be combined with Theory O strategies. But unless they're carefully handled, melding E and O is likely to bring the worst of both theories and the benefits of neither. Indeed, the corporate changes we've studied that arbitrarily and haphazardly mixed E and O techniques proved destabilizing to the organizations in which they were imposed. Managers in those companies would certainly have been better off to pick either pure E or pure O strategies—with all their costs. At least one set of stakeholders would have benefited.

The obvious way to combine E and O is to sequence them. Some companies, notably General Electric, have done this quite successfully. At GE, CEO Jack Welch began his sequenced change by imposing an E-type restructuring. He demanded that all GE businesses be first or second in their industries. Any unit that failed that test would be fixed, sold off, or closed. Welch followed that up with a massive downsizing of the GE bureaucracy. Between 1981 and 1985, total employment at the corporation dropped from 412,000 to 299,000. Sixty percent of the corporate staff, mostly in planning and finance, was laid off. In this phase, GE people began to call Welch "Neutron Jack," after the fabled bomb that was designed to destroy people but leave buildings intact. Once he had wrung out the redundancies, however, Welch adopted an O strategy. In 1985, he started a series of organizational initiatives to change GE culture. He declared that the company had to become "boundaryless," and unit leaders across the corporation had to submit to being challenged by their subordinates in open forum. Feedback and open communication eventually eroded the hierarchy. Soon Welch applied the new order to GE's global businesses.

Unfortunately for companies like Champion, sequenced change is far easier if you begin, as Welch did, with Theory E. Indeed, it is highly unlikely that E would successfully follow O because of the sense of betrayal that would involve. It is hard to imagine how a draconian program of layoffs and downsizing can leave intact the psychological contract and culture a company has so patiently built up over the years. But whatever the order, one sure problem with sequencing is that it can take a very long time; at GE it has taken almost two decades. A sequenced change may also require two CEOs, carefully chosen for their contrasting styles and philosophies, which may create its own set of problems. Most turnaround managers don't survive restructuring—partly because of their own inflexibility and partly because they can't live down the distrust that their ruthlessness has earned them. In most cases, even the best-intentioned effort to rebuild trust and commitment rarely overcomes a bloody past. Welch is the exception that proves the rule.

To thrive and adapt in the new economy, companies must simultaneously build up their corporate cultures and enhance shareholder value; the O and E theories of business change must be in perfect step.

So what should you do? How can you achieve rapid improvements in economic value while simultaneously developing an open, trusting corporate culture? Paradoxical as those goals may appear, our research shows that it is possible to apply theories E and O together. It requires great will, skill—and wisdom. But precisely because it is more difficult than mere sequencing, the simultaneous use of O and E strategies is more likely to be a source of sustainable competitive advantage.

One company that exemplifies the reconciliation of the hard and soft approaches is ASDA, the UK grocery chain that CEO Archie Norman took over in December 1991, when the retailer was nearly bankrupt. Norman laid off employees, flattened the organization, and sold off losing businesses—acts that usually spawn distrust among employees and distance executives from their people. Yet during Norman's eight-year tenure as CEO, ASDA also became famous for its atmosphere of trust and openness. It has been described by executives at Wal-Mart—itself famous for its corporate culture—as being "more like Wal-Mart than we are." Let's look at how ASDA resolved the conflicts of E and O along the six main dimensions of change.

Explicitly confront the tension between E and O goals. With his opening speech to ASDA's executive team—none of whom he had met—Norman indicated clearly that he intended to apply both E and O strategies in his change effort. It is doubtful that any of his listeners fully understood him at the time, but it was important that he had no conflicts about recognizing the paradox between the two strategies for change. He said as much in his maiden speech: "Our number one objective is to secure value for our shareholders and secure the trading future of the business. I am not coming in with any magical solutions. I intend to spend the next few weeks listening and forming ideas for our precise direction. . . . We need a culture built around common ideas and goals that include listening, learning, and speed of response, from the stores upwards. [But] there will be management reorganization. My objective is to establish a clear focus on the stores, shorten lines of communication, and build one team." If there is a contradiction between building a high-involvement organization and restructuring to enhance shareholder value, Norman embraced it.

Set direction from the top and engage people below. From day one, Norman set strategy without expecting any participation from below. He said ASDA would adopt an everyday-low-pricing strategy, and Norman unilaterally determined that change would begin by having two experimental store formats up and running within six months. He decided to shift power from the headquarters to the stores, declaring: "I want everyone to be close to the stores. We must love the stores to death; that is our business." But even from the start, there was an O quality to Norman's leadership style. As he put it in his first speech: "First, I am forthright, and I like to argue. Second, I want to discuss issues as colleagues. I am looking for your advice and your disagreement." Norman encouraged dialogue with employees and customers through colleague and customer circles. He set up a "Tell Archie" program so that people could voice their concerns and ideas.

Making way for opposite leadership styles was also an essential ingredient to Norman's—and ASDA's—success. This was most clear in Norman's willingness to hire Allan Leighton shortly after he took over. Leighton eventually became deputy chief executive. Norman and Leighton shared the same E and O values, but they had completely different personalities and styles. Norman, cool and reserved, impressed people with the power of his mind—his intelligence and business acumen. Leighton, who is warmer and more people oriented, worked on employees' emotions with the power of his personality. As one employee told us, "People respect Archie, but they love Allan." Norman was the first to credit Leighton with having helped to create emotional commitment to the new ASDA. While it might be possible for a single individual to embrace opposite leadership styles, accepting an equal partner with a very different personality makes it easier to capitalize on those styles. Leighton certainly helped Norman reach out to the organization. Together they held quarterly meetings with store managers to hear their ideas, and they supplemented those meetings with impromptu talks.

Focus simultaneously on the hard and soft sides of the organization. Norman's immediate actions followed both the E goal of increasing economic value and the O goal of transforming culture. On the E side, Norman focused on structure. He removed layers of hierarchy at the top of the organization, fired the financial officer who had been part of ASDA's disastrous policies, and decreed a wage freeze for everyone—management and workers alike. But from the start, the O strategy was an equal part of Norman's plan. He bought time for all this change by warning the markets that financial recovery would take three years. Norman later said that he spent 75% of his early months at ASDA as the company's human resource director, making the organization less hierarchical, more egalitarian, and more transparent. Both Norman and Leighton were keenly aware that they had to win hearts and minds. As Norman put it to workers: "We need to make ASDA a great place for everyone to work."

Plan for spontaneity. Training programs, total-quality programs, and top-driven culture change programs played little part in ASDA's transformation. From the start, the ASDA change effort was set up to encourage experimentation and evolution. To promote learning, for example, ASDA set up an experimental store that was later expanded to three stores. It was declared a risk-free zone, meaning there would be no penalties for failure. A cross-functional task force "renewed," or redesigned, ASDA's entire retail proposition, its organization, and its managerial structure. Store managers were encouraged to experiment with store layout, employee roles, ranges of products offered, and so on. The experiments produced significant innovations in all aspects of store operations. ASDA's managers learned, for example, that they couldn't renew a store unless that store's management team was ready for new ideas. This led to an innovation called the Driving Test, which assessed whether store managers' skills in leading the change process were aligned with the intended changes. The test perfectly illustrates how E and O can come together: it bubbled up O-style from the bottom of the company, yet it bound managers in an E-type contract. Managers who failed the test were replaced.

Let incentives reinforce change, not drive it. Any synthesis of E and O must recognize that compensation is a double-edged sword. Money can focus and motivate managers, but it can also hamper teamwork, commitment, and learning. The way to resolve this dilemma is to apply Theory E incentives in an O way. Employees' high involvement is encouraged to develop their commitment to change, and variable pay is used to reward that commitment. ASDA's senior executives were compensated with stock options that were tied to the company's value. These helped attract key executives to ASDA. Unlike most E-strategy companies, however, ASDA had a stock-ownership plan for all employees. In addition, store-level employees got variable pay based on both corporate performance and their stores' records. In the end, compensation represented a fair exchange of value between the company and its individual employees. But Norman believed that compensation had not played a major role in motivating change at the company.

Use consultants as expert resources who empower employees. Consultants can provide specialized knowledge and technical skills that the company doesn't have, particularly in the early stages of organizational change. Management's task is figuring out how to use those resources without abdicating leadership of the change effort. ASDA followed the middle ground between Theory E and Theory O. It made limited use of four consulting firms in the early stages of its transformation. The consulting firms always worked alongside management and supported its leadership of change. However, their engagement was intentionally cut short by Norman to prevent ASDA and its managers from becoming dependent on the consultants. For example, an expert in store organization was hired to support the task force assigned to renew ASDA's first few experimental stores, but later stores were renewed without his involvement.

By embracing the paradox inherent in simultaneously employing E and O change theories, Norman and Leighton transformed ASDA to the advantage of its shareholders and employees. The organization went through personnel changes, unit sell-offs, and hierarchical upheaval. Yet these potentially destructive actions did not prevent ASDA's employees from committing to change and the new corporate culture because Norman and Leighton had won employees' trust by constantly listening, debating, and being willing to learn. Candid about their intentions from the outset, they balanced the tension between the two change theories.

By 1999, the company had multiplied shareholder value eightfold. The organizational capabilities built by Norman and Leighton also gave ASDA the sustainable competitive advantage that Dunlap had been unable to build at Scott Paper and that Sigler had been unable to build at Champion. While Dunlap was forced to sell a demoralized and ineffective organization to Kimberly-Clark, and while a languishing Champion was sold to UPM-Kymmene, Norman and Leighton in June 1999 found a friendly and culturally compatible suitor in Wal-Mart, which was willing to pay a substantial premium for the organizational capabilities that ASDA had so painstakingly developed.

In the end, the integration of theories E and O created major change—and major payoffs—for ASDA. Such payoffs are possible for other organizations that want to develop a sustained advantage in today's economy. But that advantage can come only from a constant willingness and ability to develop organizations for the long term combined with a constant monitoring of shareholder value—E dancing with O, in an unending minuet.

Change Theories in the New Economy

HISTORICALLY, THE STUDY OF change has been restricted to mature, large companies that needed to reverse their competitive declines. But the arguments we have advanced in this article also apply to entrepreneurial companies that need to manage rapid growth. Here, too, we believe that the most successful strategy for change will be one that combines theories E and O.

Just as there are two ways of changing, so there are two kinds of entrepreneurs. One group subscribes to an ideology akin to Theory E. Their primary goal is to prepare for a cash-out, such as an IPO or an acquisition by an established player. Maximizing market value before the cash-out is their sole and abiding purpose. These entrepreneurs emphasize shaping the firm's strategy, structure, and systems to build a quick, strong market presence. Mercurial leaders who drive the company using a strong top-down style are typically at the helm of such companies. They lure others to join them using high-powered incentives such as stock options. The goal is to get rich quick.

Other entrepreneurs, however, are driven by an ideology more akin to Theory O—the building of an institution. Accumulating wealth is important, but it is secondary to creating a company that is based on a deeply held set of values and that has a strong culture. These entrepreneurs are likely to subscribe to an egalitarian style that invites everyone's participation. They look to attract others who share their passion about the cause—though they certainly provide generous stock options as well. The goal in this case is to make a difference, not just to make money.

Many people fault entrepreneurs who are driven by a Theory E view of the world. But we can think of other entrepreneurs who have destroyed businesses because they were overly wrapped up in the Theory O pursuit of a higher ideal and didn't pay attention to the pragmatics of the market. Steve Jobs's venture, Next, comes to mind. Both types of entrepreneurs have to find some way of tapping the qualities of theories E and O, just as large companies do.

Originally published in May–June 2000
Reprint R00301

Turning Goals into Results

The Power of Catalytic Mechanisms

JIM COLLINS

Executive Summary

MOST EXECUTIVES HAVE a big, hairy, audacious goal. They write vision statements, formalize procedures, and develop complicated incentive programs—all in pursuit of that goal. In other words, with the best of intentions, they install layers of stultifying bureaucracy. But it doesn't have to be that way.

In this article, Jim Collins introduces the *catalytic mechanism,* a simple yet powerful managerial tool that helps translate lofty aspirations into concrete reality. Catalytic mechanisms are the crucial link between objectives and performance; they are a galvanizing, nonbureaucratic means to turn one into the other.

What's the difference between catalytic mechanisms and most traditional managerial controls? Catalytic mechanisms share five characteristics. First, they produce desired results in unpredictable ways. Second, they

distribute power for the benefit of the overall system,
often to the discomfort of those who traditionally hold
power. Third, catalytic mechanisms have teeth. Fourth,
they eject "viruses"—those people who don't share the
company's core values. Finally, they produce an ongoing effect.

Catalytic mechanisms are just as effective for reaching individual goals as they are for corporate ones. To
illustrate how catalytic mechanisms work, the author
draws on examples of individuals and organizations that
have relied on such mechanisms to achieve their goals.
The same catalytic mechanism that works in one organization, however, will not necessarily work in another.
Catalytic mechanisms must be tailored to specific goals
and situations. To help readers get started, the author
offers some general principles that support the process of
building catalytic mechanisms effectively.

Most executives have a big, hairy, audacious
goal. One dreams of making his brand more popular
than Coke; another aspires to create the most lucrative
Web site in cyberspace; yet another longs to see her organization act with the guts necessary to depose its arch
rival. So, too, most executives ardently hope that their
outsized goals will become a reality. To that end, they
write vision statements, deliver speeches, and launch
change initiatives. They devise complicated incentive
programs, formalize rules and checklists, and pen policies and procedures. In other words, with the best intentions, they create layer upon layer of stultifying bureaucracy. Is it any surprise that their wildly ambitious
dreams are seldom realized?

But companies don't have to act that way. Over the past six years, I have observed and studied a simple yet extremely powerful managerial tool that helps organizations turn goals into results. I have recently codified it; I call it the *catalytic mechanism*.

Catalytic mechanisms are the most promising devices executives can use to achieve their big, hairy, audacious goals.

Catalytic mechanisms are the crucial link between objectives and performance; they are a galvanizing, nonbureaucratic means to turn one into the other. Put another way, catalytic mechanisms are to visions what the central elements of the U.S. Constitution are to the Declaration of Independence— devices that translate lofty aspirations into concrete reality. They make big, hairy, audacious goals reachable.

My research indicates that few companies—perhaps only 5% or 10%—currently employ catalytic mechanisms, and some of them aren't even aware that they do. I have also found that catalytic mechanisms are relatively easy to create and implement. Given their effectiveness, they are perhaps the most underutilized—and most promising—devices that executives can use to achieve their big, hairy, audacious goals, or BHAGs. (For more on BHAGs, see "Anatomy of a BHAG" at the end of this article.)

Consider Granite Rock, a 99-year-old company in Watsonville, California, that sells crushed gravel, concrete, sand, and asphalt. Twelve years ago, when brothers Bruce and Steve Woolpert became copresidents, they gave their company a new BHAG. Granite Rock would provide total customer satisfaction and achieve a reputation for service that met or exceeded that of Nordstrom, the upscale department store that is world famous for delighting its customers. Not exactly a timid goal for a stodgy, family-owned company whose employees are mostly tough, sweaty people operating rock quarries and whose customers—mainly tough, sweaty construction workers and contractors—are not easily dazzled.

Now stop and think for a minute: What would it take to actually reach such an ambitious goal? Most people automatically think of galvanizing leadership. But that wasn't an option for Granite Rock, as the Woolperts are a quiet, thoughtful, and bookish clan. Nor did the answer lie in hosting hoopla events or launching grand customer service initiatives. The brothers had seen such efforts at other companies and believed they had little lasting effect.

They chose instead to implement a radical new policy called "short pay." The bottom of every Granite Rock invoice reads, "If you are not satisfied for any reason, don't pay us for it. Simply scratch out the line item, write a brief note about the problem, and return a copy of this invoice along with your check for the balance."

Let me be clear about short pay. It is not a refund policy. Customers do not need to return the product. They do not need to call and complain. They have complete discretionary power to decide whether and how much to pay based on their satisfaction level.

To put the radical nature of short pay in perspective, imagine paying for airline tickets after the flight and having the power to short pay depending on your travel experience—not just in the air, but during ticketing and deplaning as well. Or suppose universities issued tuition invoices at the end of the semester, along with the statement, "If you are not satisfied with the dedication of the professor in any course, simply scratch out that course and send us a tuition check for the balance." Or suppose your cell phone bill came with a statement that said, "If you are not satisfied with the quality of connection of any calls, simply identify and deduct those from the total and send a check for the balance."

In the years since it was instituted, short pay has had a profound and positive impact on Granite Rock. It serves as a warning system, providing hard-to-ignore feedback about the quality of service and products. It impels managers to relentlessly track down the root causes of problems in order to prevent repeated short payments. It signals to employees and customers alike that Granite Rock is dead serious about customer satisfaction in a way that goes far beyond slogans. Finally, it keeps Granite Rock from basking in the glory of its remarkable success.

And it has had success, as has been widely reported. The little company—it has only 610 employees—has consistently gained market share in a commodity business dominated by behemoths, all the while charging a 6% price premium. It won the prestigious Malcolm Baldrige National Quality Award in 1992. And its financial performance has significantly improved—from razor-thin margins to profit ratios that rival companies like Hewlett-Packard, which has a pretax return of roughly 10%. No doubt, short pay was a critical device for turning the Woolpert brothers' BHAG into a reality.

Five Parts of a Whole

Obviously, not every company should institute short pay. Rather, companies should have catalytic mechanisms as powerful as short pay. What, then, is the difference between a catalytic mechanism and most traditional managerial devices, such as a company's hiring and compensation policies? Catalytic mechanisms share five distinct characteristics. (See the chart "Catalytic Mechanisms: Breaking from Tradition.") Let's look at them in turn.

Catalytic Mechanisms: Breaking from Tradition

Catalytic mechanisms share five distinct characteristics that distinguish them from traditional controls.

A traditional managerial device, control, or mechanism. . . .	A catalytic mechanism. . . .	Examples of catalytic mechanisms
reduces variation as it enlarges the organization's bureaucracy.	produces desired results in unpredictable ways.	The red flag made a ferociously opinionated CEO listen to the challenge of an M.B.A. student—improving the knowledge of the whole class, despite the unexpected nature of the exchange.
concentrates power in the hands of authorities who can force people to obey their commands.	distributes power for the benefit of the overall system, often to the great discomfort of those who traditionally hold power.	A new government rule allowed a low-level manager to expunge an immensely wasteful regulation that required nearly new uniforms to be burned.
is understood by employees and executives alike as merely an intention.	has a sharp set of teeth.	Short pay at Granite Rock allows customers to pay only for the products that satisfy them.
attempts to stimulate the right behaviors from the wrong people.	attracts the right people and ejects viruses.	At W.L. Gore & Associates, employees can, in effect, fire their bosses, ensuring nonhierarchical leadership.
has the short-lived impact of a single event or a fad.	produces an ongoing effect.	Kimberly-Clark knowingly put itself into head-to-head competition with Procter & Gamble to impel better performance in the consumer goods marketplace. Such a strategy is still working 30 years later.

Characteristic 1: A catalytic mechanism produces desired results in unpredictable ways. When executives identify a bold organizational goal, the first thing they usually do is design a plethora of systems, controls, procedures, and practices that seem likely to make it happen. That process is called alignment, and it's wildly popular in the world of management, among business academics and executives alike. After all, alignment makes sense. If you want to make your brand more popular than Coke, you had better measure the effectiveness of advertising and reward successful marketing managers with big bonuses. But the problem, as I've said, is that the controls that undergird alignment also create bureaucracy, and it should be news to no one that bureaucracy does not breed extraordinary results.

Don't get me wrong. Bureaucracy may deliver results, but they will be mediocre because bureaucracy leads to predictability and conformity. History shows us that organizations achieve greatness when people are allowed to do unexpected things—to show initiative and creativity, to step outside the scripted path. That is when delightful, interesting, and amazing results occur.

Take 3M. For decades, its executives have dreamed of having a constant flow of terrific new products. To achieve that end, in 1956, the company instituted a catalytic mechanism that is by now well known: scientists are urged to spend 15% of their time experimenting and inventing in the area of their own choice. How very unbureaucratic! No one is told what products to work on, just how much to work. And that loosening of controls has led to a stream of profitable innovations, from the famous Post-it Notes to less well-known examples such as reflective license plates and machines that replace the functions of the human heart during surgery.

3M's sales and earnings have increased more than 40-fold since instituting the 15% rule. The mechanism has helped generate cumulative stock returns 36% in excess of the market and has earned the company a frequent ranking in the top ten of *Fortune's* most-admired list.

In a happy coincidence, the variation sparked by catalytic mechanisms forces learning to occur. Suppose you set out to climb the 3,000-foot sheer rock face of El Capitan in Yosemite Valley. Once you pass pitch 15, you cannot possibly retreat from your particular route: you are, by dint of nature, 100% committed. Although you can't predict *how* you will overcome the remaining pitches—you have to improvise as you go—you can predict that you will invent a way to the top. Why? Because the reality of having no easy retreat forces you to reach the summit. Catalytic mechanisms have the same effect. Granite Rock's short pay commits the company to achieving complete customer satisfaction. Every time a customer exercises short pay, Granite Rock learns or invents a way to run its operations more effectively. Ultimately, such new knowledge leads to better results, making the catalytic mechanism part of a virtuous circle of variation, learning, improvement, and enhanced results.

My "red flag" device also illustrates that circle. When I first began teaching Stanford M.B.A. students by the case method in 1988, I noticed that a small number of them tended to dominate the discussion. I also noticed that there was no correlation between the degree of vocal aggressiveness and how much these students improved the class's overall learning experience. Some vocal students had much to contribute; others just liked to hear themselves talk. Worse, I noticed when chatting with students after class that some of the quieter individuals had significant contributions but were selective or shy about sharing them. Furthermore, seeing 15 to 20 hands raised at a time, I had no way of knowing which one represented a truly significant insight, and I sensed that I was frequently missing some students' one best contribution for the entire quarter.

I solved that problem by giving each student an 8.5 inch by 11 inch bright red sheet of paper at the beginning of every quarter. It had the following instructions: "This is your red flag for the quarter. If you raise your hand with your red flag, the classroom will stop for you. There are no restrictions on when and how to use your red flag; the decision rests entirely in your hands. You can use it to voice an observation, share a personal experience, present an analysis, disagree with the professor, challenge a CEO guest, respond to a fellow student, ask a question, make a suggestion, or whatever. There will be no penalty whatsoever for any use of a red flag. Your red flag can be used only once during the quarter. Your red flag is nontransferable; you cannot give or sell it to another student."

I had no idea precisely what would happen each day in class. And yet, the red flag device quickly created a better learning experience for everyone. In one case, it allowed a very thoughtful and quiet student from India to challenge Anita Roddick on the Body Shop's manufacturing practices in the Third World. Roddick, a charismatic CEO with ferociously held views, usually dominates any discussion. The red flag forced her to listen to a critic. The spirited interchange between these two passionate and well-informed people produced more learning than anything I could have scripted. Without the red flag, we would have just had another session of "I'm CEO and let me tell you how it is."

In another situation, a student used her red flag to state, "Professor Collins, I think you are doing a particularly ineffective job of running class today. You are leading too much with your questions and stifling our independent thinking. Let us think for ourselves." That was a tough moment for me. My BHAG as a professor was to create the most popular class at the business school while imposing the highest workload and the stiffest daily standards. The red flag system confronted me with the fact that my own questioning style stood in the way of my dream—but it also pointed the way to improvement, again, to everyone's benefit.

Interestingly, no other professors on campus adopted the red flag. One of them told me, "I can't imagine doing that. I mean, you never know what might happen. I could never give up that much control in my classroom." What he and others missed was a great paradox: by giving up control and decreasing predictability, you increase the probability of attaining extraordinary results.

Characteristic 2: A catalytic mechanism distributes power for the benefit of the overall system, often to the great discomfort of those who traditionally hold power. With enough power, executives can always get people to jump through hoops. If it is customer service they are after, for instance, they can threaten dismissal to coerce salespeople to smile and act friendly. If they seek higher profits per store, they can pay employees according to flow-through. And if increased market share is the dream, they can promote only those managers who make it happen.

But consider how catalytic mechanisms work. Short pay distributes power to the customer, to the great discomfort of Granite Rock's executives, but toward the greater goal of continuous improvement for the benefit of customers and company alike. The red flag distributes power to the students, to the great discomfort of the teacher, but to the ultimate improvement of learning in

general. The founders of the United States understood
this point when they wrote the Constitution. After all,
the Constitution is the set of catalytic mechanisms that
reinforce and support the national vision. Voting, the
system of checks and balances, the two-thirds vote to
amend, the impeachment process—these disperse power
away from one central source, to the great discomfort of
those who seek power, but to the benefit of the overall
nation.

Catalytic mechanisms force the right things to happen even though those in power often have a vested
interest in the right things *not* happening. Or they have a
vested interest in inertia—letting pointless, expensive
practices stay in place. That's what happened for years,
perhaps decades, at U.S. Marine recruit depots. All
recruits are issued a uniform on their first day. Two
weeks later, they need another—the pounds melt away
when you run 12 miles every dawn. The military's rules
required those two-week-old uniforms to be destroyed.
Not washed and reissued, but destroyed.

In the early 1990s, Phil Archuleta, a materials manager at a recruiting depot in San Diego, suggested that
they reuse the uniforms.
His boss's response: "No.
It's against regulations.
Forget about it." So in a
fabulous act of insubordi-
nation, Archuleta washed
the uniforms, hid them in
boxes, and bided his time until he finally got a supervisor
willing to challenge the regulation.

*Catalytic mechanisms
subvert the default knee-jerk
tendency of bureaucracies
to choose status quo
over change.*

In an effort to empower the Phil Archuletas of the
world, the government launched a wide-ranging initiative in 1994 to fix its bureaucratic quagmire. A new rule

regarding waivers was put in place, and it is a catalytic mechanism that exemplifies the beauty and power of redistributing power. It has two primary components:

- Waiver-of-regulation requests must be acted upon within 30 days. After 30 days, if no answer is forthcoming, the party asking for the waiver can *assume approval* and implement the waiver.

- Those officials who have the authority to change regulations can approve waiver requests, but *only the head of an agency* can deny a request.

Think for a minute about the impact of this catalytic mechanism. It subverts the default, knee-jerk tendency of bureaucracies to choose inaction over action, status quo over change, and idiotic rules over common sense. Supervisors can no longer say no or not respond. They would have to champion a no all the way to the head of their agency—the equivalent of the head commandant of the entire U.S. Marine Corps—within 30 days. Instead of having to go out of their way to demonstrate why it is a good idea, they would have to expend great energy to prove that it is a *bad* idea. The catalytic mechanism tilts the balance of power away from inertia and toward change.

Indeed, the primary effect of the new waiver rule—as with all catalytic mechanisms—is to give people the freedom to do the right thing. The waiver that allowed Archuleta to change the regulation on uniforms created a savings of half a million dollars in two years. Similar examples of people doing the right thing with the waiver rule abound throughout the federal government, from the FDA to NASA. Tort claims adjusters in the Department of Agriculture, for instance, waived regulations to reduce processing time of claims from 51 days to eight days—a manpower savings of 84%. When executives vest people with power and responsibility and step out of the way, vast reservoirs of energy and competence flow forth. Again we have a paradox: the more executives disperse power and responsibility, the more likely the organization is to reach its big, hairy, audacious goal.

Characteristic 3: A catalytic mechanism has teeth.
Lots of companies dream of total customer satisfaction; few have a device for making it happen that has the teeth of short pay. Plenty of organizations state the lofty intention to empower people; few translate that into results with a mechanism that has the teeth of the red flag. Many companies state that they intend to "become number one or number two in every competitive arena"; few have added an effective means of enforcement by saying, "and if the business is not number one or number two, or on a clear trajectory to get there, *we will exit within three months.*"

The fact is, executives spend hours drafting, redrafting, and redrafting yet again statements of core values, missions, and visions. This is often a very useful process, but a statement by itself will not accomplish anything. By contrast, a catalytic mechanism puts a process in place that all but guarantees that the vision will be fulfilled. A catalytic mechanism has a sharp set of teeth.

Consider the case of Nucor Corporation, the most successful U.S. steel company of the last three decades. It has a unique vision for a Rust Belt company: to be an organization whose workers and management share the common goal of being the most efficient, high-quality steel operation in the world, thereby creating job security and corporate prosperity in an industry ravaged by foreign competition. Behind that vision lies the belief held deeply by Nucor's senior leaders that decent, hard-working people should be well paid for their efforts and, so long as they are highly productive, that they need not worry about job security.

On the surface, Nucor's vision may sound warm and fuzzy. Dig deeper, and you'll see that it actually leaves no room for unproductive employees. Nucor has created a culture of intense productivity whereby five people do the work that ten do at other steel companies, and get paid like eight. The vision came to life through a series of powerful catalytic mechanisms with teeth, such as the way frontline workers get paid:

- Base hourly pay is 25% to 33% below the industry average.

- People work in teams of 20 to 40; team-productivity rankings are posted daily.

- A bonus of 80% to 200% of base pay, based on *team* productivity, is paid weekly to all teams that meet or exceed productivity goals.

- If you are five minutes late, you lose your bonus for the day.

- If you are 30 minutes late, you lose your bonus for the week.

- If a machine breaks down, thereby stopping production, there is no compensating adjustment in the bonus calculation.

- If a product is returned for poor quality, bonus pay declines accordingly.

You might be thinking that the Nucor system concentrates power in the hands of management, which would seem to contradict the idea of distributing power for the sake of the system. But in fact, the catalytic mechanism actually takes the power out of the hands of individual managers and their whims. Nucor has no discretionary bonuses. It's more like a sports bonus system: if you score so many points or win a certain number of races, you get a bonus based on a predetermined formula. Period. That formula gives workers more power over their own destiny than bonus programs that give large discretionary power to management. If your team scores the points, your team gets the bonus, and no manager can take it away, citing, "We're just not having a very good year" or "I don't like your attitude."

Nucor's catalytic mechanisms for managers, incidentally, have even sharper teeth. Its executive compensation system works very much like its worker compensation system, except that the "team" is the entire plant (for plant managers) or the entire company (for corporate officers). And, unlike most companies, when times are bad, Nucor's executives assume greater pain than frontline workers: workers' pay drops about 25%, plant managers' pay drops about 40%, and corporate officers' pay drops about 60%. In the 1982 recession, CEO Ken Iverson's pay dropped 75%.

The old adage "People are your most important asset" is wrong. The right people are your most important asset.

Characteristic 4: A catalytic mechanism ejects viruses. A lot of traditional controls are designed to get employees to act the "right" way and do the "right" things, even if they are not so inclined. Catalytic mechanisms, by contrast, help organizations to get the right people in the first place, keep them, and eject those who do not share the company's core values.

Great organizations have figured something out. The old adage "People are your most important asset" is wrong; the *right* people are your most important asset. The right people are those who would exhibit the desired behaviors anyway, as a natural extension of their character and attitude, regardless of any control and incentive system. The challenge is not to train all people to share your core values. The real challenge is to find people who already share your core values and to create catalytic mechanisms that so strongly reinforce those values that the people who don't share them either never get hired or, if they do, they self-eject.

Let's return to the Nucor example. Nucor doesn't try to make lazy people productive. Its catalytic mechanisms create a high-performance environment in which those with an innate work ethic thrive and free riders get out in a hurry. Management usually doesn't fire unproductive workers; *workers* do. In one case, team members chased a lazy coworker out of the plant. And one reporter writing a story on Nucor described showing up for a shift on time but thinking he was late because all the workers had been there for 30 minutes arranging their tools and getting ready to fire off the starting line precisely at 7:00 a.m.

Interestingly, Nucor sets up its mills not in traditional steel towns, but primarily in rural, agricultural areas. The thinking is simple: you can't teach the work ethic— either a person has it or he doesn't. But you can teach steel making. That's why Nucor hires farmers and trains them. The company's catalytic mechanisms wouldn't have it any other way.

Another example of a catalytic mechanism ejecting viruses comes from W.L. Gore & Associates, a fabric company worth nearly $2 billion. Bill Gore founded the company in 1958 with the vision of creating a culture of natural leadership. Leadership, in Gore's view, could not be assigned or bestowed by hierarchical position. You are a leader if and only if people choose to follow you. Gore's theory sprang not just from his personal values but also from his business sense: he thought that the most creative and productive work came when people freely made commitments to one another, not when bosses told them what to do.

To turn his vision into reality, Gore invented a catalytic mechanism that attracted the right people like a magnet and scared away the others. At W.L. Gore & Associates, employees have the authority to fire their bosses. Now, they can't fire the person from the company but, if they feel their boss isn't leading them effectively, they can simply bypass him or her and follow a different leader.

Who would want to work at such a company? Exactly the people who belong there—people who know they can lead without the crutch of a formal position or title and who believe in the philosophy of nonhierarchical leadership. Who would avoid it like the plague? Anyone who gets giddy pulling the levers of position and power just for the pulling's sake. And if you're a hierarchical leader who happens to make it through the company's door but can't quickly shake the notion that "the boss has to be the boss," it won't take you long to find the exit.

Characteristic 5: A catalytic mechanism produces an ongoing effect. Catalytic mechanisms differ fundamentally from catalytic events. A rousing speech to the troops, an electrifying off-site meeting, a euphoria-producing new buzzword, a new initiative or strategic imperative, an impending crisis—all of these are catalytic events, and some are useful. But they do not produce the persistent, ongoing effect of catalytic mechanisms. In fact, a good catalytic mechanism, as long as it evolves, can last for decades, as the 15% rule at 3M and the impeachment mechanism in the Constitution illustrate.

The lack of catalytic mechanisms is one reason many organizations rally in a crisis but languish once the crisis has passed. Leaders who feign a crisis—those who create a burning platform without simultaneously building catalytic mechanisms—do more long-term harm than good by creating a syndrome of crisis addiction. Executives who rely only on catalytic events are left wondering why the momentum stalls after the first phase of euphoria, excitement, or fear has passed. To produce lasting results, they must shift from orchestrating a series of events to building catalytic mechanisms.

Take, for example, the decades of ineffectual attempts to reform public education in the United States. Part of the failure lies in the approach to reform; too often it is based on onetime events and fashionable buzzwords rather than on catalytic mechanisms that produce sustained effects. As Roger Briggs, a high school teacher in Boulder, Colorado, wrote in an essay on school reform: "Every year we get a new program or fad. And they never really work. And we teachers eventually just learn to ignore them, smile, and go about our business of teaching."

Now take a look at what happened when the state of Texas started using a catalytic mechanism in 1995: comparison-band ranking of schools, which is directly tied to resource allocation and, in some cases, school closures. The ongoing effect of this device forced the momentum of reform forward. Why? Well, if you rank fifth out of 40 schools but you just sit still, you'll drop in the ratings. Sit still long enough, and you'll eventually rank 35th rather than fifth, and you may face closure. Because every school is ranked on the same criteria, the bar for performance keeps rising. Within four years of installing the mechanism, student achievement in Texas improved across the board. The percentage of students who passed the Texas math skill exam, for example, rose from roughly half to 80%, and the share of black and Hispanic students who passed doubled to 64% and 72%, respectively.

And consider the ongoing impact of a good catalytic mechanism in a more corporate setting. Darwin Smith, former CEO of Kimberly-Clark, created in 1971 the BHAG to transform Kimberly-Clark from a mediocre forest- and paper-products company into a world-class consumer goods company. At the time, Wall Street analysts scoffed at the idea, as did most of Kimberly-Clark's competitors. Smith was undeterred. He created one catalytic event and one equally important catalytic mechanism. For the first, he sold a big chunk of the company's traditional paper-production mills, thus leaving no easy escape route from the dream. For the second, he committed the company to head-to-head competition with the best consumer-products company in the world: Procter & Gamble. With its entry into disposable diapers, Kimberly-Clark would henceforth be a direct rival of P&G. Kimberly-Clark would either become excellent at consumer products or get crushed. The beauty of this catalytic mechanism is that, unlike the "change or die" ranting all too common among modern executives, its ongoing effect is as powerful today as when it was first put in place nearly 30 years ago.

Getting Started

This is not intended to be a how-to article; my main objective has been to introduce the concept of catalytic mechanisms and demonstrate how they have helped some companies—and individuals—turn their BHAGs into reality. (For more on the personal use of catalytic mechanisms, see "Not for Companies Only" at the end of this article.) Nonetheless, my research suggests that there are a few general principles that support the process of building catalytic mechanisms effectively.

DON'T JUST ADD, REMOVE

When pursuing BHAGs, our natural inclination is to add—new initiatives, new systems, new strategies, new priorities, and now, new catalytic mechanisms. But in doing so, we overwhelm ourselves. Isn't it frightening that the new version of the Palm Pilot has space for 1,500 items on its to-do list? Sadly, few of us have a "stop doing" list. We should, because to take something away—to unplug it—can be as catalytic as adding something new.

Take the case of a circuit division at Hewlett-Packard. It had tried countless programs and initiatives to reach its BHAG of becoming "a place where people would walk on the balls of their feet, feel exhilarated about their work, and search for imaginative ways to improve and innovate everything we do." The events produced short-term results—a moment of sparkle and excitement—but within a month or two, the division always drifted back into its sleepy, humdrum mode.

A catalytic mechanism should be an idiosyncratic adaptation, if not a wholesale creation, for a unique situation.

Then its executives considered the question, "What policies should we remove?" For most of its history, the division had comfortably lived off a captive internal market. What if HP's divisions were allowed to buy their components from outside competitors? Never again would the circuit division have fat internal orders just handed to it. Never again could it just sit still. Two months, four months, a year, five years, and ten years down the road—fierce competitors would still be there, constantly upping the ante. The prospect was both terrifying and exhilarating. Managers decided to unplug the "buy internal" requirement and open the doors to free-market competition.

Within weeks, the circuit division was well on its way to realizing its BHAG. You could sense a completely different environment the moment you walked in the door. The place hummed with activity, and its performance showed it.

CREATE, DON'T COPY

Creating mechanisms is exactly that: a creative act. You can, of course, get good ideas by looking at what other organizations do, but the best catalytic mechanisms are idiosyncratic adaptations, if not wholesale creations, for a unique situation.

Because catalytic mechanisms require fresh ideas, it makes sense to invite all members of an organization to participate in their creation. Everyone. Certainly, some mechanisms require input from senior executives, like short pay at Granite Rock. Yet many of the best catalytic mechanisms were not created by top management. The idea for the federal government's waiver rule, for example, originated with two staff members—Lance Cope and Jeff Goldstein. They were working in the national reinvention labs, and neither had direct authority over any federal agency.

Allow me also to use a personal example. Part of my professional vision is to contribute through teaching and to harness my curiosity and passion for learning in ways that make a positive impact on the world. From that goal flows the imperative that I allocate time primarily to research, writing, and teaching and limit consulting work only to those situations in which I can contribute as a teacher.

To reinforce that imperative, I have created two catalytic mechanisms: the "come to Boulder rule" and the "four-day rule." The first rule states that I will not engage in a direct advisory relationship with any organization unless the chief executive agrees to travel to my Boulder research laboratory. Executives spend huge sums of money on consultants, but money doesn't equal commitment—if you have a big enough budget, invoices just don't hurt. Yet all chief executives, no matter how large their budgets, have only 24 hours in a day. If a CEO flies all the way to Boulder, he or she has demonstrated commitment to serious discussions and hard work, and the likelihood that I will make a significant impact as a teacher increases exponentially. Most important, those not committed to real (and perhaps uncomfortable) change eject right up front.

The second mechanism—my four-day rule—states that any given organization has an upper limit of four days of my advisory time in a year. The most lasting impact comes by teaching people how to fish, not by fishing for them. Organizations that want an adviser to fish for them self-eject through this catalytic mechanism. Admittedly, these are highly unusual devices, and they would be disastrous for most consulting firms that depend on continuous growth to feed their machine. Yet they are perfectly designed for a strategy aimed at explicitly *not* building a large consulting business. They are unique to me, as all catalytic mechanisms should be to their creators.

USE MONEY, BUT NOT ONLY MONEY

The examples in this article may lead you to believe that most catalytic mechanisms use money. But, in fact, when my research colleague Lane Hornung cataloged my database of catalytic mechanisms, he found that only half do. That might surprise some people—in particular those who ascribe to the old saw that money is the best motivator. I'm not going to claim that money doesn't impel people toward desired results; money can add teeth to any catalytic mechanism. But to rely entirely on money reflects a shallow understanding of human behavior.

The U.S. Marine Corps illustrates my point precisely. The Corps builds extraordinary commitment through a set of catalytic mechanisms that create intense psychological bonds among its members. By isolating recruits at boot camps and creating an environment where recruits survive only by relying upon one another, the Corps triggers the deep human drive, hardwired into most of us, to support and protect those we consider family. Most people will not risk their lives for a year-end bonus, but they will go to great lengths to earn the respect and protect the well-being of their comrades.

William Manchester, who returned to his unit on Okinawa after receiving a wound that earned him a Purple Heart, eloquently describes the psychology of commitment in his book *Goodbye Darkness:*

And then, in one of those great thundering jolts in which a man's real motives are revealed to him in an electrifying vision, I understand, at last, why I jumped hospital that Sunday thirty-five years ago, and, in violation of orders, returned to the front and almost certain death. It was an act of love. Those men on the line were my family, my home. . . . They had never let me down, and I couldn't do it to them. I had to be with them rather than to let them die and me live with the knowledge that I might have saved them. Men, I now knew, do not fight for flag or country, for the Marine Corps or glory or any other abstraction. They fight for one another.[1]

Yes, catalytic mechanisms sometimes use money to add bite, but the best ones also tap deeper wells of human motivation. Even at Nucor, the effectiveness of its catalytic mechanisms lies as much in the peer pressure and the desire to not let teammates down as in the number of dollars in the weekly bonus envelope. The best people *never* work solely for money. And catalytic mechanisms should reflect that fact.

ALLOW YOUR MECHANISMS TO EVOLVE

New catalytic mechanisms sometimes produce unintended negative consequences and need correction. For instance, the first version of the red flag failed because certain students continued to dominate class discussion, thinking that every comment of theirs was worth a red flag. So I added the stipulation: "Your red flag can be used only once during the quarter. Your red flag is nontransferable; you cannot give or sell it to another student."

All catalytic mechanisms, in fact, even if they work perfectly at first, should evolve. 3M's 15% rule is a case in point. In 1956, executives urged 3M scientists to use 3M labs during their lunch break to work on anything they wanted. In the 1960s, that catalytic mechanism became formalized as the "15% rule," whereby scientists could use *any* 15% of their time. In the 1980s, the 15% rule became widely available to 3Mers other than scientists, to be used for manufacturing and marketing innovations, for example. In the 1990s, 3M's executives worried that fewer people were using the mechanism than in previous decades. It put together a task force to reinvent the 15% rule, bolstering it with special recognition rewards for those who used their "bootleg time"—as it has come to be called—to create profitable innovations.

The 15% rule has been a catalytic mechanism at 3M for more than 40 years, but it has continually evolved in order to remain relevant and effective. That's the right approach; no catalytic mechanism should be viewed as sacred. In a great company, only the core values and purpose are sacred; everything else, including a catalytic mechanism, should be open for change.

BUILD AN INTEGRATED SET

One catalytic mechanism is good; several that reinforce one another as a set is even better. That's not to say a company needs hundreds of catalytic mechanisms—a handful will do. Consider Granite Rock again. It certainly doesn't rely just on short pay. It also has a catalytic mechanism that requires an employee and manager to create a focused development plan for the employee during the performance evaluation process. Indeed, every employee and manager must together complete a form that reads: "Learn_____ so that I can contribute_____." Two sets of teeth make this form effective. First, employees and their managers must both sign off on the final development plan, which forces a continual dialogue until they reach agreement. Second, compensation ties directly to learning and improvement, not just job performance: people who do not go out of their way to improve their skills receive lower than midpoint pay. Only those who do a good job *and* improve their skills *and* make a contribution to improving the overall Granite Rock system receive higher than midpoint pay. So people who merely do a good job self-eject out of Granite Rock. This catalytic mechanism has produced delightful surprises: one previously illiterate employee used it to get the company to send him to a reading program. When Granite Rock won the Baldrige Award, he read an acceptance speech.

Granite Rock also uses catalytic mechanisms to guide hiring, encourage risk taking, and stimulate new capabilities. The point here is not so much in the details as it is in the big picture: Granite Rock does not rely solely on short pay to pursue its BHAG of attaining a reputation for customer satisfaction that exceeds Nordstrom's. It has about a dozen catalytic mechanisms that support and reinforce one another.

That said, however, it would be a mistake to take this article and launch a grand catalytic mechanism initiative. Developing a set of catalytic mechanisms should be an organic process, an ongoing discipline, a habit of mind and action. The dozen or so catalytic mechanisms at Granite Rock came into being over a ten-year period. You certainly don't want to use the idea to create another layer of bureaucracy. Catalytic mechanisms should be catalysts, not inhibitors.

Castles in the Air

I recently worked with a large retail chain to define its BHAG for the twenty-first century. The company is doing well, but it wants its performance to be outrageously great. And so its executives came up with a wildly ambitious goal: to make its brand more popular than Coke.

That company's challenge now is to invent the catalytic mechanisms that will make the dream a reality. I've advised its executives against investing heavily in hoopla events to fire up thousands of frontline employees about the new BHAG. Instead, they should create and implement a set of catalytic mechanisms—specific, concrete, and powerful devices to lend discipline to their vision. After all, catalytic mechanisms alone will not create greatness; they need a dream to guide them. But if you can blend huge, intangible aspirations with simple, tangible catalytic mechanisms, then you'll have the magic combination from which sustained excellence grows.

At the conclusion of *Walden*, Henry David Thoreau wrote: "If you have built castles in the air, your work need not be lost; that is where they should be. Now put the foundations under them." BHAGs are a company's wildest dreams. Catalytic mechanisms are their foundations. Build them both.

Anatomy of a BHAG

IN OUR RESEARCH FOR *Built to Last,* Jerry Porras and I discovered that most enduring great companies set and pursue BHAGs (pronounced BEE-hags and shorthand for big, hairy, audacious goals). There are three key characteristics of a good BHAG:

1. **It has a long time frame—ten to 30 years or more.** The whole point of a BHAG is to stimulate your organization

to make changes that dramatically improve its fundamental capabilities over the long run. Citicorp's first BHAG, set in 1915—to become the most powerful, the most serviceable, the most far-reaching world financial institution ever—took more than five decades to achieve. Its new BHAG, set in the early 1990s—to attain 1 billion customers worldwide—will require at least two decades to achieve. (Today it has less than 100 million.) BHAGs with short time frames can lead executives to sacrifice long-term results for the sake of achieving a short-term goal.

2. **It is clear, compelling, and easy to grasp.** The goal in a good BHAG is obvious, no matter how you phrase it. For example, Philip Morris's BHAG, set in the 1950s—to knock off R.J. Reynolds as the number one tobacco company in the world—didn't leave much room for confusion. I call this the "Mount Everest standard." The goal to climb Mount Everest can be said as "Climb the most famous mountain in the world" or "Climb the biggest mountain in the world" or "Climb the mountain at 87 degrees east, 28 degrees north" or "Climb the mountain in Nepal that measures 29,028 feet" or hundreds of other ways. If you find yourself spending countless hours tinkering with a statement, you don't yet have a BHAG.

3. **It connects to the core values and purpose of the organization.** The best BHAGs aren't random; they fit with the fundamental core values and reason for being of the company. For example, Nike's BHAG in the 1960s—to crush Adidas—fit perfectly with Nike's core purpose "to experience the emotion of competition, winning, and crushing competitors." Sony's BHAG in the 1950s—to become the company most known for changing the worldwide poor-quality image of Japanese prod-

ucts—flowed directly from its stated core value of elevating the Japanese culture and national status.

This last criterion connects back to the reason for having a BHAG in the first place. It is a powerful way to stimulate progress—change, improvement, innovation, and renewal—while simultaneously preserving your core values and purpose. It is this remarkable ability to blend continuity with change that separates enduring great companies from merely successful ones. The trick, of course, is not just to set a BHAG but to achieve it, and therein lies the power of catalytic mechanisms.

Not for Companies Only

MY RESEARCH HAS FOCUSED on the impact of catalytic mechanisms in organizational settings—on how they can turn a company's most ambitious goals into reality. But catalytic mechanisms can also have a powerful impact on individuals. Indeed, I have made catalytic mechanisms a fundamental part of how I manage my time, with my "come to Boulder rule" and "four-day rule."

I am not alone. Several of my former students at Stanford Business School have applied a catalytic mechanism to reach their goals. In one case, a student emerged from his courses on entrepreneurship fired up by the idea of forgoing the traditional path and striking out on his own. But as time passed and he felt the crushing burden of school debt as well as the lure of lucrative job offers, his personal vision waned. He took a job at a large, established disc drive manufacturer and promised himself, "I'm going to launch out on my own in five years when I've paid off all my school debts."

In most cases, such dreams fade as the years go by—with the advent of cars, houses, children, and all the rest. My former student, however, implemented an interesting catalytic mechanism to keep his vision alive. He drafted a resignation letter and dated it five years out. Then he gave copies of the letter to a handful of reliable people, along with the following instructions, "If I don't leave my job and launch out on my own by the specified date, then send the letter in for me." His plan worked. In 1996, I received an e-mail from him that described how he saved his money and spent his off-hours developing his entrepreneurial options. Then, right on schedule, he quit his secure job and launched a fund to buy and run his own company.

In another case, a former student created a personal board of directors composed of people he admires and would not want to disappoint, and he made a personal commitment to follow the board's guidance—it has power in his life. In 1996, he wrote me: "I recently used my personal board in deciding whether to leave Morgan Stanley and go to work with a friend in his two-year-old business. 'Yes' was the unanimous vote." So despite the risk of leaving a lucrative and prestigious position, he leapt into the small company, which has since grown fourfold to employ more than 80 people.

Consider also the highly effective catalytic mechanism that a colleague of mine has been using for the past three years to attain her BHAG: to lead a full and active life as a mother, wife, professional writer, and church volunteer, without going crazy. That part about maintaining sanity is important because before her catalytic mechanism was in place, my colleague constantly found herself overextended and miserable. The main culprit was her work as a freelance writer: she accepted too many jobs. "Even if we didn't need the money, I would still take on every project that came my way," she recalls. "Maybe because my family was so poor when I was growing up, I just found it impossible to leave money on the table." Not surprisingly, the woman's children paid the price of her constant working, as did her husband and close-knit extended family. "Either I was too exhausted to see people or else I was calling them for a baby-sitting favor," she says.

One day, my colleague was lamenting her situation to her sister, who came up with an effective catalytic mechanism. Every time the woman took on work beyond a certain level of revenue—a comfortable annual salary, in essence—she would pay her sister a $200-a-day penalty fee. My colleague, instantly seeing the wonderful impact of the plan, immediately agreed.

Since she redistributed power to her sister, my colleague has gained new control over her life. Now she happily accepts jobs up to a certain level of income, but she assesses each additional offer with newly critical eyes. (She has taken on extra work on only two occasions; both projects were too lucrative to pass up.) Indeed, the catalytic mechanism has so freed my colleague from overwork that she has taken on a new role as a volunteer at her children's school. With its undeniable bite, my colleague's catalytic mechanism will have an ongoing effect as long as she honors it. And given its results, she plans to do so for a long time.

Would any of these people have changed their lives without catalytic mechanisms? Perhaps, but I think it less likely. Personal catalytic mechanisms have all the benefits of organizational mechanisms: they put bite into good intentions, dramatically increasing the odds of actually being true to your personal vision instead of letting your dreams remain unrealized.

Notes

1. William Manchester, *Goodbye Darkness* (Boston: Little, Brown Company, 1979).

Originally published in July–August 1999
Reprint 99401

Changing the Way We Change

RICHARD PASCALE, MARK MILLEMANN,
AND LINDA GIOJA

Executive Summary

MORE AND MORE COMPANIES struggle with growing competition by introducing improvements into every aspect of performance. But the treadmill keeps moving faster, the companies keep working harder, and results improve slowly or not at all.

The problem here is not the improvement programs. The problem is that the whole burden of change typically rests on so few people. Companies achieve real agility only when every function and process—when every *person*—is able and eager to rise to every challenge. This type and degree of fundamental change, commonly called *revitalization* or *transformation,* is what many companies seek but rarely achieve because they have never before identified the factors that produce sustained transformational change.

The authors identify three interventions that will restore companies to vital agility and then keep them in good health: incorporating employees fully into the principal business challenges facing the company; leading the organization in a different way in order to sharpen and maintain incorporation and constructive stress; and instilling mental disciplines that will make people behave differently and then help them sustain their new behavior.

The authors discovered these basic sources of revitalization by tracking the change efforts of Sears, Roebuck & Company, Royal Dutch Shell, and the United States Army. The organizations used these interventions to alter the way their people experienced their own power and identity, as well as the way they dealt with conflict and learning. As at Sears, Shell, and the U.S. Army, any major shift in those four elements will create a landmark shift in any organization's operating state or culture.

M ORE AND MORE COMPANIES are trying to make a fundamental change in the way they operate. For years, they've struggled with growing competition by introducing improvements (or at least improvement programs) into every function and process. But the competitive pressures keep on getting worse, the pace of change keeps accelerating, and companies keep pouring executive energy into the search for ever higher levels of quality, service, and overall business agility. The treadmill moves faster, companies work harder, results improve slowly or not at all.

The problem is not the programs, some of which have worked wonders. The problem is that the whole burden of change typically rests on so few people. In other words, the number of people *at every level* who make committed, imaginative contributions to organizational success is simply too small. More employees need to take a greater interest and a more active role in the business. More of them need to care deeply about success. Companies achieve real agility only when every function, office, strategy, goal, and process—when every person—is able and eager to rise to every challenge. This type and degree of fundamental change, commonly called *revitalization* or *transformation,* is what more and more companies seek but all too rarely achieve.

Surveys confirm that executives have begun to give revitalization a high priority. With a few notable exceptions, however, most of their efforts to achieve it have met with frustration—partly because large organizations have such a remarkable capacity to resist change of *all* kinds, and partly because the kind of change being sought is so much more radical and uncomfortable than anything required by a shift in strategy or process or corporate structure. For that matter, corporate revitalization often includes shifts in strategy or process or structure, but revitalization means a good deal more—it means a permanent rekindling of individual creativity and responsibility, a lasting transformation of the company's internal and external relationships, an honest-to-God change in human behavior on the job. Revitalization is not incremental change. Its realizable goal is a discontinuous shift in organizational capability—a resocialization so thorough that employees feel they are working for a different company, a leap in a company's ability to meet or exceed industry benchmarks, a jump in bottom-line results.

This kind of sustained organizational renewal would not be easy even if companies had a reliable road map to make the journey a reasonable bet. As it is, most of what's been written about transformational change is either too conceptual and therefore too impractical, too inspirational and therefore too vague, or too company specific and therefore too hard to apply to one's own situation. We have been inept at transforming troubled organizations—or even at maintaining the vitality of healthy ones—because we have never before identified the factors that produce sustainable revitalization.

In essence, there are three concrete interventions that will restore companies to vital agility and then keep them in good health: *incorporating employees* fully into the process of dealing with business challenges, *leading from a different place* so as to sharpen and maintain employee involvement and constructive stress, and *instilling mental disciplines* that will make people behave differently and then help them sustain their new behavior into the future. Done properly, these three interventions will create a landmark shift in an organization's operating state or culture by significantly altering the way people experience their own *power* and *identity* and the way they deal with *conflict* and *learning.*

We discovered these sources of revitalization by tracking the change efforts, in good times and bad, of three of the world's largest organizations: Sears, Roebuck & Company, Royal Dutch Shell, and the United States Army. Sears (with $36 billion in revenues and 310,000 employees), Shell (with $100 billion in revenues and 110,000 employees), and the U.S. Army (with a $62 billion operating budget, 750,000 civilian and active-duty employees, and

Like physicians appraising their patients' health, managers can evaluate the vital signs *of organizational vigor.*

another 550,000 in the Army Reserve) share traits of size, geographical dispersion, and managerial complexity. They also share the distinction of having beaten the odds. All three have survived for 100 years or more and have retained their essential identity—they have been neither swallowed up by others nor disaggregated into fragments.

The events that triggered transformation efforts at Sears, Shell, and the army were quite different. In all three organizations, however, the 800-pound gorilla that impaired performance and stifled change was culture. The trouble is, there are as many different definitions of *culture* as there are articles on change management, and none of them give us much help in telling us how, or even what, to fix. Nevertheless, in our study of what might loosely be called *culture* at Sears, Shell, and the army, we found four distinct indicators that are highly predictive of performance in both good times and bad. These four indicators can serve managers in much the same way that vital signs serve physicians in appraising the health of the human body.

This analogy of vital signs is important. The reason so many early forms of healing failed was that practitioners were treating only the most obvious symptoms of some larger malfunctioning system they knew little or nothing about. Gradually, however, medical science identified these invisible systems, figured out how they worked, studied their interdependencies, and learned to pay close attention to key indicators of a patient's physical well-being. Today physicians begin an examination by checking these vital signs—pulse, blood pressure, pulmonary function, reflexes—to form a general but still fairly accurate impression of how each complex subsystem and the organism as a whole are faring.

Organizations have similar systems and symptoma-
tologies. Their vital signs reveal a great deal about their
overall health and adaptability, and about the strength
and vigor of their functional systems. The four vital signs
we identified at Sears, Shell, and the army give us a working definition of culture and tell us most of what we need
to know about the operating state of any company:

Power. Do employees believe they can affect organizational performance? Do they believe they have the
power to make things happen?

Identity. Do individuals identify rather narrowly with
their professions, working teams, or functional units,
or do they identify with the organization as a whole?

Conflict. How do members of the organization handle
conflict? Do they smooth problems over, or do they
confront and resolve them?

Learning. How does the organization learn? How
does it deal with new ideas?

Organizational Drift

As a result of age, size, or competitive intensity, most
organizations exhibit a deterioration in vital signs that is
inconsistent with—in fact, often destructive to—their
ambitions and purposes.

The members of start-up organizations have a sense
of individual and collective power; they feel they can
make a big difference in the pursuit of the goals they all
share. Employees identify with the enterprise as a whole;
alignment and informal teamwork are commonplace.
When conflicts occur, people handle them directly and
almost never allow them to interfere with getting things

done. The whole organization is open to learning; trial and error are the norm.

As organizations grow older and larger, however, the vigor of these four vital signs deteriorates. Instead of power, people often develop a sense of resignation in response to seemingly insurmountable obstacles or to lack of support from their superiors in the daily hassle of getting things done. As organizations become more complicated and demanding, people strive to carve out private patches of turf where they can exercise responsibility, protect themselves, and keep the world at bay. When it comes to their identity, therefore, employees lose their sense of teamwork and alignment with the entire enterprise and begin to seek the safety of their particular profession, union, function, team, or location. People in mature organizations tend to avoid conflict for fear of blame or of having someone take their disagreement personally. Alternatively, they may take part in a succession of routine collisions that lead to stalemate rather than resolution. As for learning, larger and older organizations tend to be less receptive to new ideas than their younger counterparts. In place of inquiry and experimentation, ideas get studied to death in hopes of ferreting out every possible weakness before making a commitment. The precondition for action is certain knowledge.

The Sears story is a useful illustration of a company culture's natural drift away from good health. It also illustrates one CEO's well-orchestrated but ultimately ineffective efforts to reverse the drift and another CEO's remarkable success at breathing new life into the enterprise.

Ed Brennan's 12-year tenure at Sears's helm cannot be faulted for a lack of intelligence, energy, or good intentions. He put the Sears Tower up for sale, slimmed down headquarters, and moved the central organization to an open campus in Chicago's suburbs. He called for an end to Sears's tradition of insisting that customers use only Sears credit cards. He launched Brand Central, which offered for the first time such non-Sears appliances as GE, Maytag, and Panasonic. He diversified into financial services through the acquisition of Dean Witter (for $607 million) and Coldwell Banker (for $202 million), and he invested $1 billion to launch the Discover Card. (When he spun off these assets in 1993, Sears's market capitalization had risen to $36 billion from $8 billion when he took the job, and the cumulative profit from financial services had accounted for approximately two-thirds of Sears's consolidated earnings for the preceding five years.) Brennan also did his best to rebuild Sears as a retail store. He reduced employment by 48,000 jobs, simplified logistics, moved into women's apparel, took steps to streamline the buying organization, and piloted new formats such as stand-alone automotive outlets, as well as home-furnishing and home-improvement stores. But it was Brennan's successor, Arthur Martinez, who became famous for revitalizing the retail side of Sears.

CEO Martinez saw that Sears's culture was as strategic as its product and market initiatives.

Where Brennan fell down—in contrast to Martinez—was in failing to grapple with the Sears culture; that is, Brennan failed to address the deterioration of the company's vital signs. Unlike Martinez, he never quite came to terms with the insight that culture was as strategic as his product and market initiatives were, and that fixing the vital signs would go a long way toward fixing the company.

When Martinez took over in 1992, few employees had any sense of power; most felt nothing but resignation. As one regional manager put it, "It was a company of 'salute and obey.' Directives came from above, and we did our best to follow them. There was no maneuvering room to make sensible market decisions. As bad press began in the 1970s, there was widespread depression and an unwillingness to admit at cocktail parties that we worked at Sears. It all seemed so big and complex and out of control. We felt defeated and powerless."

In terms of identity, Sears had drifted a long way from the vibrancy that prevailed from its founding in 1880 through 1956, when General Robert Wood retired as its fourth CEO. For much of that period, the central buying staff and equally strong territory managers kept each other honest through a system of checks and balances. Beginning in the mid-1950s, however, a succession of caretaker CEOs allowed this precise tension between the field and the home office to degenerate into an empty ritual. Territory managers ran their stores like baronies and stonewalled strategic direction from above. This tilt toward regional fragmentation and a more local identity unquestionably contributed to Sears's inability to respond early to the threats posed by Wal-Mart and Toys-R-Us. "Too small to worry about" or "Not a problem in my region" were the typical reactions.

Brennan tried to correct the excesses of decentralization but pushed the pendulum too far back in the opposite direction. He eliminated the position of territory manager along with most other echelons in the regional hierarchy. Once-powerful store managers were relegated to "keeping the lights on and the doors open," as one store manager put it. "As a result, our knowledge at the fingertips was lost. Executive management ushered in an era of drive-by merchandising. Experts from headquarters would visit a store three times a month and would believe they understood your local market better than you did."

Under enormous pressure to meet their performance targets and threatened by further layoffs, store management teams hunkered down and concentrated on their own turf. As a consequence, the stores became a merchandising hodgepodge, and poor service and frequent out-of-stock conditions alienated customers. Many of Brennan's efforts to achieve sweeping change snagged in the concertina wire of the stores' defensive perimeters. Brennan was trying to build a companywide identity by edict. Predictably, the center did not hold, and the effort failed. In the fallout, identity fragmented more than ever as people everywhere in the company looked out for themselves.

The third of Sears's vital signs to show serious deterioration was its capacity for constructive conflict. The company's initial operating model was built on a vibrant tension between home and regional offices. This struggle between policy from headquarters and inventive execution at the stores was mediated by a succession of four very strong and accessible CEOs whose careers spanned the first 76 years of Sears's history. These men were not threatened by conflict; they encouraged and harnessed it. But by the time Ed Brennan succeeded to the chairmanship, the former mix of initiatives and controls had long since given way to compliance and acquiescence. Pushing back or resisting directives meant "not being a team player."

As for learning, Sears had drifted to the most extreme condition of denial and complacency. Negative reports by business analysts beginning in 1974 were interpreted at Sears as bad journalism and unfair treatment. In 1990, when Sears was accused of widespread dishonesty in its automotive repairs (a sting operation by the State of California Consumer Affairs Department found fraud in 85% of its visits to Sears Auto Centers, and 44 states subsequently filed suit), Brennan's first line of defense was

The first step toward restoring organizational vitality is to engage every employee in the company's principal challenges.

to deny all allegations and to stonewall. An even more troubling example: Sears began including Wal-Mart among its competitor benchmarks only in 1992, by which time Wal-Mart was 60% larger than Sears. Sears's strongly inbred culture was deeply implicated in this capacity for denial. Throughout Brennan's tenure, only one of 100 top executives had a non-Sears career background. "Sears is different" or "We tried that once and it didn't work" were frequent responses to new ideas.

Incorporating Employees

Sears, Shell, and the U.S. Army are currently engaged in efforts to revitalize their organizations. All three are doing their best to transform the way their people experience power, identity, conflict, and learning. All three, in one fashion or another, are using the same three interventions to achieve this improvement in their vital signs.

The first intervention is to incorporate employees into the activity of the organization. This is not the same as communicating or motivating or rolling out plans hatched at the top. It is resocialization. It means engaging employees as meaningful contributors (not just doers) in the principal challenges facing the enterprise. It means seeing employees as volunteers who decide each day whether or not to contribute the extra ounce of discretionary energy that will differentiate the enterprise from its rivals. Although incorporation shares DNA with such familiar ideas as consensus management, employee involvement, and self-managed teams, it is something more. Its distinct properties include the use of concrete, pressing business problems to generate a sense of urgency; the cascading involvement of every employee beginning at the very top of the enterprise and continuing down through the ranks; and the generation of initiatives conceived and staffed by employees across hierarchy and function.

We can see one leader's efforts to reverse drift through incorporation in the turnaround of Shell Malaysia. Its British chairman, Chris Knight, had the benefit of three career rotations in Malaysia prior to his appointment as chairman. When he arrived in 1992, he saw that the organization was in trouble. The company was overstaffed; traditional revenues from oil and gas were in decline; service standards with wholesale customers were in disarray; and the once-dormant government-owned oil company, Petronas, had become an aggressive competitor in the vehicle-fuel market.

Knight wanted to build a much more agile and less costly enterprise, but he had watched several predecessors try and fail to alter Shell Malaysia's vital signs. Most employees felt that as the largest private oil company in the country, Shell should try not to make waves. This ultraconservative philosophy led employees to avoid any deviation from usual practice and stifled in the cradle any impulse to use their power of initiative. Within a cocoon of comfortable oligopoly, their identity was located in small, defensible silos. Refining quarreled with transport, and everyone fought the crazy ideas that came

from marketing and sales, but all these conflicts were
distinctly muted. Malaysian employees are from cultures
sensitive to saving face and therefore tend to approach
impasses by highly circuitous routes. "Smooth and
avoid" was the norm. Finally, there was little learning.
Knight observed a frustrating lack of concern, even of
curiosity, when competitor Caltex gobbled up 10% of
domestic market share.

For more than a year, Knight tried to achieve authen-
tic alignment among his eight-person executive team.
Somehow, the goal always eluded his grasp. In exaspera-
tion, he scheduled an incorporation event in Kuching,
Borneo, and asked all 260 of Shell's senior and midlevel
managers to attend.

The leader of a middle-management strategic-
initiative team kicked off the two-and-a-half-day meeting with a brief presentation of two key proposals aimed
at repositioning Shell and regaining competitive advantage. The first proposal envisioned a daring partnership
with Shell's biggest competitor, Petronas, in order to
engage in joint procurement, thus lowering costs for
both companies and putting their competitors at a dis-
advantage. The second proposal was to streamline and
improve Shell's ragged relationships with its 3,000 fran-
chised service stations by creating a single point of contact in a customer service center.

Assembled in small groups, the managers were then
asked to identify the soft spots in these strategic proposals. When the entire assembly reconvened, some groups
suggested improvements from the floor, but on balance
there was general agreement with the proposals. The
next step was an organizational audit. Each of several
large teams of participants took one facet of the company—strategy, structure, systems—and described how

it affected current performance and the impact it might have on the two proposals. When these analyses were shared in plenary session, it was evident to most people that Shell's operating practices would seriously compromise the new initiatives. Over the course of the meeting, many of Knight's management cadre became aware of the emerging competitive pressures affecting the company and were mobilized to take part in developing a response. Such mobilization is the aim of any well-designed incorporation process.

Just below the surface of this off-site meeting, another development was taking place. As lower-level managers gained firsthand knowledge of business priorities and saw where the chairman wished to take the company, the vast majority of them bought into the plan, which left obstructionist senior managers isolated and exposed. One senior British expatriate, recognizing that his hand had been called, chose the final ten minutes of the meeting to air his differences with the chairman publicly. Knight dismissed him 48 hours later—a firing heard round the world of Shell, where this sort of thing was never done.

But the firing raises an obvious question: How does dismissal for disagreement fit together with the notion of encouraging constructive conflict? Knight's position was that he fired the man not for disagreeing but for never disagreeing in the previous 13 months of high-level discussions or at any time during the meeting except in the concluding minutes. Moreover, most Shell employees— at least those in Malaysia—accepted this explanation. Rather than create a fear of openness, the termination of an executive widely seen as an opponent of change was regarded as a defining moment in the progress of the broader involvement and deeper commitment that is incorporation.

Incorporation doesn't begin and end with one off-site meeting, however uplifting it might be. Knight's next move was to sponsor one-day events called *valentines*, a name and concept that he borrowed from Ford. In these exercises, gatherings of 100 salaried and hourly employees split into smaller groups of peers from each of the major functional units within the downstream organization—refining, logistics, engineering, customer service, accounting, and so forth. At issue was the new concept proposed in the second strategic initiative outlined in Kuching—the customer service center. Knight's goal was, first, to give customers a single point of contact with Shell through a toll-free number and, second, to empower the customer service center to break logjams and satisfy customer needs. The second of these twin objectives was the wolf in sheep's clothing. It is easy enough to recruit an around-the-clock staff of operators to cover a toll-free number. It is quite another matter to shift organizational power so radically that customer-service-center representatives will be able to break deadlocks and redeploy resources. This is the stuff over which organizational blood is spilled—and a challenge that did not play into the historical strengths of Shell's downstream functions.

In the valentines exercise, people air conflicts and struggle toward a robust resolution.

The valentines exercise is a vehicle for conflict resolution. Each functional team is required to write a succinct description of its grievances with any of the other teams in the room, pinpointing what it does to inhibit productivity and what is likely to get in the way of a successful customer-service center. When each group has received, say, half a dozen of these valentines, its members are given time to sift and discuss them, and then to select two issues they think particularly important to resolve. The group then gets two hours to come up with, first, a detailed plan for corrective action that it can implement within 60 days; second, the name of a member of its own team who will be accountable for delivering the action; and third, the name of a so-called committed partner from the team that sent the valentine who will share responsibility for making the new solution work.

Back in plenary session, each person assigned an action stands and explains the grievance and the proposed solution, and names the team's nominee for committed partner—often the individual seen as most likely to sabotage the proposal and therefore the person most essential to its success. The committed partner then stands, and a fascinating negotiation unfolds. Tension mounts, and the room falls silent. With coaching from the facilitator, the two principals air conflicts and express their deep-seated distrust of each other's motives. A robust solution is the usual result.

Making good use of these and other techniques, Shell Malaysia reversed its ten-year drift. It fostered a new level of individual power, a new sense of identity with the enterprise as a whole, a new kind of open and productive conflict, and a new appetite for learning that persists to this day.

Leading from a Different Place

An organization coming unfrozen under an overload of experimentation and new ideas is a terrifying thing for traditional leaders. Matters seem out of control, which to a degree they are. But as leaders weather this storm, they begin to undergo a shift in mind-set. From thinking, "I've got to stay in control" or "This is too fast," they develop an ability to operate outside their comfort zone and accept ambiguity and adversity as a part of the design. The second of the three interventions—a new approach to leadership—requires them to establish focus and urgency, maintain healthy levels of stress, and not feel compelled to come to the rescue with a lot of answers. They learn to stay the course until guerrilla leaders at lower levels come forward with initiatives that address the company's shortcomings.[1]

Arthur Martinez did precisely all these things at Sears. And from the very beginning, he did one important thing that Brennan had not done: he began telling the truth. For seven successive years, retail executives at Sears had lied to themselves. They set annual goals and came back at year's end below plan. The targets were set lower each time around, but they were never low enough. Market surveys showed Sears perilously close to breaking its last remaining links with its retail customers. It was the Sears credit card, delivering 70% of the profits, that was carrying the retail group. All of this was painful to face. Martinez held up the mirror.

To generate a sense of urgency, Martinez set difficult goals. Within two years, Sears would quadruple its margins to achieve industry parity, reverse its loss of market share, and improve customer satisfaction by 15%. Then came the hard part. Like Sears under Brennan, most organizations are submerged in their numbing but familiar lethargy, their somnambulant operating state. It's like being stirred from your dreams by a strange noise in the night: in the fog of semiconsciousness, one part of you struggles to focus on whether it's an intruder or the cat; but another part resists the possibility of bad news and struggles to go back to sleep. Similarly, people in organizations resist undertakings that would pull them from their familiar world. When a leader raises an issue and generates urgency around it, the guaranteed first line of defense is for the organization to turn back to the leader for an answer. "We need a plan . . . more direction . . . more resources" are the words to this predictable refrain. Many leaders take the bait. Martinez did not. He refused to give his team of top-level managers the answers, and the authenticity of his refusal was powerful. He didn't *have* the answers. No one did. Sears's management had to create the answers on the basis of what Martinez did provide—which was truth, urgency, and enough productive stress to alter thinking and behavior.

Leading from a different place always requires resocialization of the kind Martinez achieved at Sears. Nowhere is the transformational power of resocialization more evident than at three highly unusual U.S. Army training centers—at Fort Irwin, California; Fort Polk, Louisiana; and Hoenfelds, Germany. In fact, the training is sufficiently remarkable to have been studied by the chief education officers at Shell, Sears, Motorola, and GE, and by senior delegations from every country in Western Europe, Russia, and most nations of Asia, Latin America, and the Middle East. Perfected over the past 15 years, the training is widely recognized to have almost single-handedly transformed the army, the largest employer in the United States.

Over a grueling two-week period, an entire organizational unit of 3,000 to 4,000 people goes head-to-head with a competitor of like size in a simulation so realistic that no participant comes away unscathed. The exercise often alters forever the way executives—in this case, army officers—lead. Critical to its impact is a cadre of 600 instructors, one assigned to every person with leadership or supervisory responsibilities. These *observer/controllers,* as they are called, shadow their counterparts through day after 18-hour day of intense activity. They provide personal coaching and facilitate a nonhierarchical team debriefing called an After Action Review (AAR), in which participants struggle to understand what went wrong and how to correct their shortcomings. These AARs are in fact the focal point of an organizational exercise that can range across 650,000 acres (at Fort Irwin in the Mojave Desert) and cost $1 million a day.

For many, the juxtaposition of *U.S. Army* with words like *revitalization, experimentation,* and *nonhierarchical* amounts to a contradiction in terms. But that view is out of date. According to General Gordon R. Sullivan, the army's recently retired chief of staff, "The paradox of war in the Information Age is one of managing massive amounts of information and resisting the temptation to overcontrol it. The competitive advantage is nullified when you try to run decisions up and down the chain of command. All platoons and tank crews have real-time information on what is going on around them, the location of the enemy, and the nature and targeting of the enemy's weapons system. Once the commander's intent is understood, decisions must be devolved to the lowest possible level to allow these frontline soldiers to exploit the opportunities that develop."

Leading from a different place means resisting the temptation to provide the answers. Solutions must come from the ranks.

A number of factors have contributed to the army's extraordinary, sustained transformation, including higher-quality soldiers, one outcome of a volunteer army. But inside and outside observers agree that the

National Training Command (NTC) has been the crucible in which it has all come together. Since the NTC was established, the army's more than half a million men and women in uniform have rotated through its programs several times—most upper-, mid-, and lower-level officers and NCOs, five times. As one officer put it, "The NTC experience leaves no room for debate. Day after day, you are confronted with the hard evidence of discrepancies between intentions and faulty execution, between what you wanted the enemy to do and what he actually did."

Leading from a different place requires great resolve both to stay the course and to resist the temptation to provide the answer. The solutions, and the commitment to deliver on them, must come from the ranks. Leaders must maintain the pressure until followers see that *they* are going to have to make things happen, until guerrilla leaders step forward and begin to engage in leaderlike acts.

Leading from a different place also requires leaders to stand squarely in the zone of discomfort and ambiguity.

Not everyone is a guerrilla leader, but sustained stress will eventually produce enough such leaders to begin shifting the tide of vital signs.

Leading from a different place also entails a transformation in the operating state of leaders themselves. They become a microcosm of the shift in vital signs that they want to see in their organizations. From resigning themselves to the limits of their power to make things happen (and to the implausibility of expecting middle managers to help), they move toward the possibility of genuinely distributed intelligence; from taking on an identity as the person in charge, they become clearinghouses for the different ways an enrolled organization handles its responsibilities; from avoiding straight talk, they develop an ability to handle and even encourage constructive conflict; from assuming that they must provide a detailed road map for the journey, they begin to accept learning as a form of inquiry in action. Leaders must place themselves squarely in the zone of discomfort and learn to tolerate ambiguity. We are all much more likely to act our way into a new way of thinking than to think our way into a new way of acting, and that is the essence of leading from a different place.

Instilling Mental Disciplines

We know that when incorporation slackens or vanishes—as it did at Sears for a long time before Martinez or in the army before and during Vietnam—stagnation and entropy are almost invariably the results. We have seen at Sears, Shell, and the U.S. Army that incorporation combined with a different type of leadership was able to reverse an organization's drift and restore its cultural vitality. But if an organization is to change the way its people think and act and interact, and if this resocialization is not to evaporate the moment financial results improve and people start to believe the worst is over, then people must internalize a set of principles or disciplines that shape their reactions and govern their behavior. Disciplines of this kind might also be called enduring social patterns, but they are a good deal more than unconscious habits. Habits are automatic and therefore mindless. Disciplines are mindful. We can see these disciplines at work in the After Action Review, which constitutes the heart of the NTC experience.

Each afternoon, the commander of the brigade undergoing training receives an assignment, such as "penetrate enemy defenses" or "defend your sector against a

superior force." Inside crowded command tents, 30 to 40
staff officers and senior fighting-unit commanders study
the situation and endeavor to hammer out a winning
strategy. Later that afternoon, this strategy begins to fil-
ter out to 3,000 soldiers dispersed across many square
miles of rugged terrain. Tank crews and platoons are
briefed, minefields laid, artillery and helicopters coordinated, reconnaissance initiated. Commencing at mid-
night, both friendly and enemy probes get under way.

By dawn, the day's battle is in full swing. The "enemy"
(the 11th Armored Cavalry Regiment) is permanently
stationed at Fort Irwin. It knows the terrain, behaves
unpredictably, and almost always devastates the unit in
training. And all the action is recorded. Perched on
mountaintops, powerful video cameras zoom in on the
hot spots. An elaborate laser-based technology precisely
tracks when and where each weapon is fired, electroni-
cally disabling any fighting unit that is hit. Audiotapes
record communication and confusion over the voice network. By 11 a.m., the outcome has been decided, and
within 90 minutes, the observer/controllers have pulled
each combat team together near terrain that has been
pivotal in its piece of the battle.

Let us take a closer look at an AAR in progress.[2] A
company team of two platoons with two tanks, four armored personnel carriers, and an HMMV (the modern
version of a jeep) have pulled into a tight circle under
the shade of a desert outcropping. The crews lean back
against tank treads, a flip chart slung over the HMMV
antenna. The fighting is in its fifth day. Exhaustion is
evident. The observer/controller has created a sand
table on the ground, a miniature of the terrain in which
this unit was annihilated in the day's battle. He asks a
gunnery sergeant to come forward, position the com-

pany's armor on the sand table, and explain the unit's mission.

Sergeant: Our overall mission was to destroy the enemy at objective K-2.

Observer/Controller: Why was this important? What was your tank's particular role in all this?

Sergeant: I'm not sure.

Observer/Controller: Can anyone help?

A trickle of comments gradually builds into a flood of discussion. It begins to appear that only the lieutenant in charge understood the mission. There had been no coordination of individual tanks and vehicles, and none had been given a particular sector in which to concentrate its fire. No one had understood that the unit's main task was to drive the enemy column away from a weak point in the defenses and into a zone where it would be within range of friendly tanks and artillery.

Key lessons for the next day are recorded on the flip chart. The soldiers all come away with a picture of what they were involved in but could not see. Each soldier has contributed to a composite grasp of the engagement, supplemented by video clips and hard data from the observer/controller. Day after day, particular themes are reinforced: all members of the unit must understand the big picture; they all need to *think*; they must always put themselves in the shoes of an uncooperative enemy; they must prepare to the point that surprise will no longer surprise them; they must set aside hierarchy, exercise self-criticism, work as a team.

"The After Action Review has democratized the army," says Brigadier General William S. Wallace, current commander of the NTC. "It has instilled a discipline of relent-

lessly questioning everything we do. Above all, it has reso-
cialized three generations of officers to move away from a
command-and-control style of leadership to one that
takes advantage of distributed intelligence. It has taught
us never to become too wedded to our script for combat
and to remain versatile enough to exploit the broken
plays that inevitably develop in the confusion of battle."

The success of the NTC experience and the After
Action Review is the result of carefully designed impera-
tives that can be applied in any organization or corporation. First, take a team of people who must work together
across functions and hierarchies and immerse it in a pro-
longed, intense learning experience. Have the team take
on a very tough project or a very tough competitor. Under
the right conditions, stress and exhaustion will unfreeze
old patterns of behavior and create an opening for new
understanding and behavior to take root. Second, in order
to eliminate subjectivity and debate, collect hard data on
what has transpired. Let the data, not the trainers, point
the finger. Third, utilize highly skilled facilitators who
have a deep knowledge of what they are observing. Never
criticize. Use Socratic questioning to evoke self-discovery.
Fourth, do not evaluate performance. The experience is
not about success or failure. It is about how much each
individual can learn. Make it safe to learn.

There are seven disciplines embedded in the After
Action Review, and all seven are as relevant in business
as they are in combat.

1. Build an intricate understanding of the business.

An organization's members do best when line-of-sight
understanding bridges the gap between overall strategy
and individual performance. This is harder than it looks.
On the one hand, troops need to understand the principal aims of each engagement ("move to establish contact

but don't precipitate an all-out fight" or "block the
enemy at this line but don't commit to a counterattack")
and how it fits into the larger strategic context. On the
other hand, soldiers need solid individual skills. Both
requirements are essential. The idea is to prevent soldiers from behaving like automatons. They are not there
simply to obey orders but to apply their skills and intelligence to a larger goal.

The first requirement—conveying the big picture to
the small unit—is easy to overlook in the heat of preparing for battle. In the AAR close-up above, we saw how
the lieutenant commanding the armored unit had
neglected to communicate the big picture and how his
men then failed to achieve a goal of which they were
unaware. To carry out the second requirement, developing individual areas of expertise, the army has borrowed
a concept from the total quality movement and has dis-
tilled all the facets of a military action down to three: the
key *tasks* involved, the *conditions* under which each task
may need to be performed, and the acceptable *standards*
for success. (For example, at a range of 2,000 yards, hit an
enemy tank moving at 20 miles per hour over uneven terrain at night with an 80% success rate.)

Sears has shown an exemplary grasp of this discipline.
To convey the larger strategic picture to every employee,
the company uses learning maps—large murals with
elaborate legends on the
borders—to communi-
cate essential business
conditions to small
groups of employees
working with a facilita-
tor. One map takes peo-

*Frank exchanges are
not likely to occur if enlisted
men are holding back
out of deference to their
superiors.*

ple through the shifts in the competitive environment
from 1950 to 1990. Another map, laid out like a game,

asks employees to place bets on the sources and uses of funds as they flow from customers' wallets to the bottom line. Sears then asks its employees to use what they've absorbed from the learning maps to come up with a list of three or four highly practical actions that can be taken immediately at the store level to correct deficiencies and improve customer service.

Sears anchors the proficiency side of this discipline with training to improve its interface with customers, then adds performance measures that focus attention on individual and team performance with respect to customer satisfaction. Together, these initiatives enable employees to perform to high standards and to understand how they each contribute to Sears's success.

2. Encourage uncompromising straight talk. The AAR is predicated on a frank exchange among soldiers as they sort through the confusion of battle and figure out where things went wrong. Such an exchange will not occur if people are showing deference to their superiors or holding back for fear of hurting someone's feelings. As we noted earlier, observer/controllers are skilled at using objective data to point the finger—fostering healthy give-and-take and creating a safe environment for candor.

Sears practiced this discipline from the top down (Martinez helped his top-level managers confront the truth about Sears's past performance) and from the bottom up (town hall meetings cultivated a new and much more straightforward style of communication). We also saw Shell Malaysia emphasize this discipline with its valentines exercise.

3. Manage from the future. Hardship for its own sake is clearly not the army's intention, but attaining excellence can be painful. Be All That You Can Be is more than the army's recruiting slogan. It challenges every element of the institution—from the private soldier to the logistics command—to stretch itself. Being all you can be is not a destination to be reached but a mind-set to manage from.

Organizations often "use up" their future, and that is precisely what happened to the U.S. Army after the highwater mark of World War II, to Sears after General Wood's retirement, and to Shell in the 1980s. Once the members of an organization believe they have reached the future, they begin to codify their past successes. Drift and loss of vitality follow "winning formulas" of this kind just as surely as night follows day.

The most essential aspect of managing from the future is to alter the institution's point of view. We all tend to look toward the future as a distant goal. By contrast, this discipline means internalizing some future goal so the institution can plant its feet in that future and manage the present from there. At Shell Malaysia, Knight inherited a company that had used up its future, a company content to keep a low profile as it tried to avoid further market-share losses to Caltex, Mobil, and Petronas.

Observer/controllers hammer on the benefits of controlled failure until soldiers embrace setbacks as windows to learning.

Knight shifted this mind-set entirely, asserting that the future of the industry was regional, not national. He insisted that Shell and Petronas needed to join forces and make Malaysia the dominant low-cost player in Southeast Asia. Once this perspective was accepted as a valid view of the future, a stream of beneficial results flowed from it for both companies.

4. Harness setbacks. NTC participants know from the outset that they are fighting an enemy far tougher than any they are likely to meet in the field. Observer/controllers remind them daily that their maneuvers are not about winning but about learning. Harnessing setbacks is a matter of recontextualizing failure, treating breakdowns as breakthroughs, seeing defeat as opportunity. But this requires considerably more self-discipline than most managers realize. Human beings are hardwired to react adversely to mistakes by blaming themselves (guilt or shame), others (finger-pointing), or bad luck (resignation and fatalism). Day after day, observer/controllers hammer on the benefits of controlled failure until every soldier learns to embrace setbacks as windows to learning.

This discipline has been directly applied at Sears, where Gus Pagonis (one in a long line of increasingly sought-after U.S. Army generals who have landed top corporate posts) heads Sears's far-flung logistics empire. Pagonis has brought the entire AAR process directly to Sears. Daily sessions of 10 to 12 employees representing every level from warehouse to headquarters scrutinize 24-hour updates on late or wrong shipments and chip away at corrective action.

5. Promote inventive accountability. The tasks, conditions, and standards in the first discipline create the benchmarks of acceptable performance, and soldiers are trained to meet or exceed these benchmarks so that their units can count on them in combat. But there is more to it than that. Close battles are won by exploiting the enemy's broken plays. Mastery of a combat assignment requires not just replicable skills but also the capacity to improvise. Observer/controllers single out and reward creative acts of initiative that are built on a solid platform of proficiency.

The new emphasis on "the softer side of Sears" has brought the company into competition with Nordstrom, which, according to Martinez, sets the world standard in striking the proper tension between improvisation and accountability. Nordstrom encourages inventiveness with the motto Respond to Unreasonable Customer Requests (for example, delivering an over-the-phone purchase to a frantic customer at the airport who is about to catch a plane). Salespeople keep scrapbooks of their heroics in providing exceptional service, and these heroics figure into promotions and storewide recognition. On the accountability side, each department tracks the sales per hour of each salesperson and posts the information publicly every two weeks—from the top of the list (worst) to the bottom (best). A sales associate unable to meet a threshold level of sales on a three-month rolling average is dismissed—an infrequent occurrence, since topping the list several times in a row leads most poor performers to move on of their own free will.

6. Understand the quid pro quo. Organizational agility and the disciplines that sustain it make enormous demands on people. Organizations must make sure that their members receive commensurate returns. Once upon a time, corporations were like ocean liners. Anyone fortunate enough to secure a berth cruised right through to disembarkation at retirement. In return for loyalty, sacrifice, and the occasional aggravating boss, employees at Sears, Shell, and the army, among others, enjoyed implicit or explicit job security.

We have now witnessed a decade of continuous job attrition in which companies have downsized, delayered, reengineered, and out-sourced. From 1980 to 1996, Sears has laid off more than 100,000 employees. The U.S. Army has reduced its ranks by 300,000 soldiers from a high of 1.2 million during the Gulf War. Worldwide, Shell has cut 150,000 jobs since 1980.

Employees must understand where the enterprise is going and have some say in its destiny.

Understanding the quid pro quo is a demanding discipline. A genuinely transformational employment contract has four levels—three more than the reward-and-recognition that was once considered adequate. The second level is employability—the training and skills that enhance people's marketability. Valuable as this element of the contract may be over the long run, it is nevertheless overrated as an incentive. Enhanced employability will inspire no one to offer the kind of deep, creative commitment and enthusiasm that companies struggling for revitalization so badly need. Employee involvement at that level cannot be bought or enticed, and it is not likely to emerge naturally from the individualistic, transactional employment contracts that are typical for many kinds of credentialed experts and specialists.

It takes more than compensation and employability to produce transformational participation. It also takes a sense of meaning in the work strong enough to generate intrinsic satisfaction. And finally, employees must understand where the enterprise is going and have some say in shaping its destiny. Shell, Sears, and the army are all wrestling with these four components of the quid pro quo. In the army, the AAR is the engine of a powerful learning and resocialization experience, driven in part by people's clear perception that defending their country is important work. Senior officers take part in more dramatic changes of perception than their juniors; but even the lowest-ranking soldier has a hand, day after day, in altering the army's culture and, ultimately, its destiny.

7. Create relentless discomfort with the status quo. The After Action Review is based on the notion that individuals can improve—in most cases, improve dramatically—on everything they do. Observer/controllers continually reinforce the notion that AAR disciplines can be applied elsewhere to other activities, and a protocol like the AAR does tend to get under a person's skin. Soldiers carry the ideas back to their home bases. Once internalized, the discipline of relentless discomfort begins to reveal itself in repeated, gnawing questions: How can we do this still better (faster, cheaper)? Is there a radical new approach that we haven't thought of yet? Day in and day out, throughout the army, the AAR format and disciplines are employed to critique performance and to make improvements as soldiers and employees at every level begin to see acceptable performance levels as insufficient for sustained vitality.

Sears and Shell struggle to turn episodic attention to improvement into a vigorous daily discipline. Among their benchmarks is USAA, long a top performer in the insurance industry. USAA has adopted a practice it calls "painting the bridge"—a reference to the fact that the task is never complete. (As soon as painters on the Golden Gate or any other large bridge finish the job, it's time to go back and start over.) In brief, an independent team of 14 organizational experts starts at one end of USAA and works its way to the other, one unit at a time. Its mission is to work with departmental teams and question everything they do. Is the role teams perform necessary? Can it be streamlined or improved? Can the team be merged with another unit? Can it be eliminated? Not surprisingly, people in the company have ambivalent feelings about this once-every-two-year regimen. But it reliably delivers improvements and, equally important, reinforces USAA's unending effort to become a better company.

Researchers at the Harvard Business School recently tracked the impact of change efforts among the *Fortune* 100. Virtually all these companies implemented at least one change program between 1980 and 1995, but only 30% of those initiatives produced an improvement in bottom-line results that exceeded the company's cost of capital, and only 50% led to an improvement in market share price. This discouraging result was not for lack of trying. On average, each of the companies invested $1 billion in change programs over the 15-year period.[3]

Frustration with such results is naturally widespread because the effort and the outcome are so hugely disproportionate. Or to be more precise, the effort of some people in a company is so much greater than the outcome for all. The solution is to focus on the *all*, to shift the attention from incremental change to the tools that can transform the attitudes and behavior of every last employee.

Notes

1. See Ronald A. Heifetz and Donald L. Laurie, "The Work of Leadership" (HBR January–February 1997).

2. The following description is taken from a video presentation of an After Action Review at Fort Irwin, titled

Mojavia: In Pursuit of Agility (New York: Marc Gerstein Associates, 1997).

3. Nitin Nohria, "From the M-form to the N-form: Taking Stock of Changes in the Large Industrial Corporation" (Harvard Business School Working Paper 96-054).

Originally published in November–December 1997
Reprint 97609

This article is based on research and consulting work carried out jointly with CSC Index.

Racing for Growth

An Interview with
PerkinElmer's Greg Summe

HOLLIS HEIMBOUCH

Executive Summary

BY THE TIME GREG SUMME joined EG&G in 1998, the company badly needed to shed the weight of past glories and rediscover the technological innovation that had been at its heart. An alumnus of McKinsey & Company and a veteran of GE and AlliedSignal, Summe, 43, saw may strengths but no strategic coherence. "When you put the parts together," he says in this detailed interview, "you didn't get a more valuable whole."

First as president and COO and later as chairman and CEO, Summe applied a cool rationalism to the company's strategy and paid close attention to preparing its people for a new competitive environment. The result, less than three years later, is PerkinElmer, a high-tech darling whose stock has more than tripled since Summe's arrival.

The first task, he says, was establishing more ambitious performance goals, specific metrics and rewards, and more accountability. The company also consolidated its 31 businesses into four strategic business units, integrated sales forces, shifted production to the Far East, developed a corporatewide materials-purchasing program, and raised profit and growth goals. It established four rigorous, corporatewide processes: goal setting to drive strategy; a leadership and organizational review to develop talent; an annual operating plan to set performance goals; and a procurement, quality, and productivity program for continuous improvement.

Summe provides details of PerkinElmer's training initiatives and describes how the company sought a new community of Wall Street analysts, allowing it to reach a broader base of growth-oriented investors.

If you had to choose a two-word description for the company Greg Summe joined in 1998, it would be "couch potato." While other technology companies soared to new heights, EG&G seemed to be channel surfing from a comfortable old chair, idly wondering from time to time what all the commotion was about. Fifty years and some 90 acquisitions after its founding in 1947 by three MIT professors, EG&G had become diversified to the point of confusion. With most of its business in low-margin technical services for the U.S. government—from program management for the Navy's nuclear submarine fleet to incinerating the Army's chemical weapons stockpile in Utah—EG&G badly needed to shed the weight of past glories and rediscover the technological innovation that had originally been the heart of the company.

Summe's task, first as president and COO and, a year later, as chairman and CEO, was nothing less than to reinvent the company. An alumnus of McKinsey & Company and a veteran of GE and AlliedSignal, where he had run several aerospace and industrial divisions, Summe, 43, is a cool rationalist, a disciplined manager, and the kind of person who would rather head out the door for a lunchtime run than amble over to the cafeteria. His energy and clarity of purpose contrasted sharply with EG&G's make-do culture.

Just over two and a half years later, Summe leads a company that has become a hot ticket. Not only does EG&G have a new name—PerkinElmer—but it has also been revamped from an old-economy dullard into a high-tech darling. It has shed ten businesses, completed seven acquisitions, and reorganized its remaining businesses into four distinct business units. Early results are promising: PerkinElmer's stock has more than quadrupled since Summe's arrival, its operating margin has nearly doubled, and its organic growth rate has jumped from zero to nearly 12%.

In this interview, conducted at PerkinElmer's corporate headquarters in Wellesley, Massachusetts, Summe describes the theory and practice behind that perennial question: how do you radically transform an organization? For PerkinElmer, the answer was to prune its business portfolio and prepare its people for a new competitive environment. PerkinElmer's story, though still unfolding, illustrates the inevitable controlled chaos that accompanies a mad dash to the future.

Let's go back to February 1998. You were suddenly in charge of a company that needed major fixing. How did you spend those first few months on the job?

I got out in the field. I knew I had to spend time with each of the businesses—learning about their operations, their customers, and their people. I saw a good, proud company with a number of real strengths that could be built on. We had footholds in some high-growth markets such as life sciences and digital imaging. We had strong financial controls and a healthy balance sheet. We had good relationships with our employees and a strong reputation with our customers. We had reasonably high-quality products.

EG&G had become a holding company for 31 diverse businesses. When you put the parts together, you didn't get a more valuable whole.

But there were problems. We had an inconsistent operating performance, a weak reputation with investors, a highly fragmented organization, and many businesses with uncertain prospects. In essence, EG&G had become a holding company for 31 diverse businesses with 31 different cultures and brands. There was a lot of good technology in the businesses, but there was no strategic coherence. When you put the parts together, you didn't get a more valuable whole.

We also had a people problem. The company's top executives were experienced, but some of them just didn't have the right skills. Many of the executives had come up through the government services business, where the pace and priorities were simply incompatible with the direction we wanted to go in. Other managers' skills were underdeveloped or too narrow as a result of the managers having worked in one role in one EG&G business for a long time. So while the company had made an intellectual commitment to move out of the government contracting business and into fast-paced commercial markets, its people were having a hard time making the leap.

With that kind of dire situation, where did you start?

We had to earn the right to grow. EG&G had a long track record of erratic financial performance, and as a result, we lacked credibility among investors. Initially, our focus was on improving our ability to deliver strong and consistent earnings. We knew that if we couldn't gain the trust of the financial markets, we wouldn't be able to get the resources—and the tolerance from investors—we needed in order to shift our portfolio into higher-growth businesses. (For more on EG&G's name change, see "And Now for Something Completely Different" at the end of this article.)

The first task, then, was to establish a new culture, one with more ambitious performance goals, specific performance metrics and rewards, and clearer accountability. We also made a series of hard decisions in order to create a more efficient operation. We consolidated our 31 businesses into five strategic business units (SBUs), integrated sales forces, shifted production to the Far East, developed a corporatewide materials-purchasing program, and raised our goals for profit and growth. We put in place four rigorous corporatewide processes that had been used effectively at GE and AlliedSignal: strategic goal setting to drive strategy; a leadership and organizational review to develop talent; an annual operating plan to set performance goals and commitments; and a procurement, quality, and productivity program for continuous improvement. We offset the onetime charges involved in this restructuring through onetime gains from the sale of several businesses, including two mechanical businesses, Sealol and Rotron. The results look good. Our operating margin, which was less than 6% in 1997, now exceeds 11%. Even more important, we have consistently met or beaten our financial commitments for the past 12 quarters.

Once we had our operations in good shape, we moved to the next phase of transformation, which was remaking our portfolio. That involved narrowing our strategic focus through divesting ourselves of underperforming and nonstrategic businesses. It also involved acquiring attractive new businesses that built critical mass in our highest-growth markets.

We used two criteria to evaluate our existing businesses. First was market leadership: could the business become one of the top three players in its industry or market? Second was growth potential: could the business produce double-digit revenue growth on an annual basis? If the answer to either question was no, the business became a candidate for divestiture. As we went through this exercise, it became clear that four of the five business units had the potential to meet our criteria: life sciences, instruments, optoelectronics, and fluid sciences. The fifth SBU, government services, was profitable and well managed, and historically it had been EG&G's core strength. But it operated in a low-margin, consolidating, declining market. Clearly, it didn't match the new criteria, so in August 1999, we sold all of the government services business. This was a difficult and emotional decision—it was like giving up half of the family—but we recognized that we wouldn't be able to pursue the other goals we had established unless we were willing to let go of that aspect of EG&G's heritage.

Do you continue to reexamine the mix of businesses within each of the remaining SBUs?

Absolutely. We continue to apply the same screening criteria to each of the major product lines—upgrading the mix by "weeding and seeding" the garden in each SBU. The healthier your portfolio, the more selective you have to be about what's in it.

For example, in our optoelectronics business, we started with nine different businesses and brands but quickly narrowed our focus to just three segments: specialty illumination, digital imaging, and telecommunications. We accomplished this by consolidating product lines; selling two lower-growth specialty semiconductor businesses, Judson and IC Sensors; and acquiring Lumen Technologies, a maker of specialty illumination products. We are now one of the market leaders in both the specialty illumination and imaging segments, which together account for 80% of the division's revenues. In our tele-communications segment, while we're not yet one of the top three in the market, we've been able to achieve an annual revenue growth rate of more than 100%.

Acquisitions such as the recent purchase of NEN Life Sciences and PE's Analytical Instruments Division have been fundamental to your attempt to build critical mass within the most attractive market segments. How would you describe your acquisitions philosophy?

Acquisitions are designed to quickly provide us with complementary products, technologies, and geographic coverage. We have made seven key acquisitions since 1998: one in optoelectronics, one in fluid sciences, two in instruments, and three in life sciences.

In optoelectronics, the acquisition of Lumen Technologies provided two key benefits. It contributed a set of complementary specialty illumination products, which are used, for instance, in endoscopy and semiconductor lithography. It also allowed us to expand our operating margins, because we were able to shift the majority of manufacturing operations from the United States to lower-cost facilities in China, Singapore, Indonesia, and the Philippines. In fluid sciences, we acquired Belfab, a maker of seals for ultrahigh-vacuum semiconductor equipment, which extended our reach beyond the aerospace industry into a higher-growth industry with a different market cycle. Yet the technology and manufacturing operations in the two sectors are very similar. The acquisition of PE Corporation's Analytical Instruments gave us a premier brand name, a customer franchise, and a global sales and distribution network that covers 100 countries. Six months later, we acquired Vivid Technologies, a maker of advanced explosives detection systems. Together, these acquisitions have made us number one in the world in explosives detection systems, such as those used behind the scenes in airports around the world, and one of the top three in analytical instruments.

The situation in life sciences was different. There we wanted to build market share quickly in two attractive areas. We were already a leader in genetic-disease screening (neonatal and prenatal testing), and we had a good position in research tools for discovering new drugs.

Divestitures are just as important as acquisitions. I'm a big believer in an "invest or divest" mentality.

We acquired Isolab, a maker of genetic screening reagents; Life Science Resources, a maker of drug discovery instruments; and just recently NEN Life Sciences, a leader in reagents and consumables for drug discovery. We're now the world's third-largest provider of drug discovery tools and the leader in neonatal and prenatal testing, with reagents and consumables now generating 75% of the SBU's revenues. At the same time, we have de-emphasized our position in clinical diagnostics. With recent reductions in research and development spending, it now accounts for about 10% of revenues, down from 40% a few years ago.

We also look for acquisition synergy across the businesses, such as in integrating sales networks, technology, or materials purchasing across SBUs. We also see opportunities to further develop our leadership talent by providing cross-functional or cross-business assignments. Finally, we look for opportunities to balance funding cycles, so that when one business experiences a market downturn or goes into heavy investment mode, we can look to other segments to counteract those effects.

But divestitures are just as important as acquisitions. I'm a big believer in an "invest or divest" mentality. Keeping low-growth product lines in a holding pattern diminishes their potential and drags down your revenue-growth rates. The major portfolio challenge in these acquisitions and divestitures is, how do you divest yourself of low price-to-earning businesses and acquire high P/E businesses at the same time without diluting your earnings per share? We have been able to offset the divestiture dilution by increasing productivity actions in our base businesses. On the acquisitions side, all of our deals until NEN have been accretive in the first year. The NEN acquisition is dilutive on a GAAP basis but accretive on a cash EPS basis. In very high-growth markets, like drug discovery tools and fiber-optic components, the significant P/E premium makes GAAP dilution almost unavoidable. We probably couldn't have done the NEN acquisition a year ago without our stock price being punished. But at this stage, our investors understand and support our strategy to upgrade the portfolio.

You talk a great deal about management talent as a valuable resource—about the need to provide challenges for highly talented managers. How did you get your people to lead change rather than resist it?

The fact is, you have to let go of those who can't or won't change, bring in new people to help accelerate change, and—this is the toughest part—convert and improve the core of the organization: the people who want to drive change but may not have all the necessary skills.

We knew recruiting talent for the senior ranks would be a challenge, given EG&G's steady-as-she-goes reputation. That's why we had to create jobs that were highly leveraged, both in their responsibilities and in their compensation packages. We also shifted power away from the corporate center to each of the business units. The corporate center became responsible for only a limited number of shared services such as benefits administration, public company functions, and coordination of the four corporatewide processes. That allowed us to reduce our corporate staff from 140 people in 1998 to 65 people today. In the units, it allowed us to create jobs that were bold enough to attract the competitive and experienced executives we needed. On the compensation side, we backed up our desire for fast-paced growth with a new performance-based stock program for corporate officers. Vesting is based on three years of consecutive EPS growth of 15% or more, but if the EPS growth is 50% or greater, the stock vests in two years.

Basically, we've created a new organization, starting with the senior management group. We've reduced the number of officers from 15 to ten; nine are new to the position, and seven are from the outside. If you look at our top 100 employees, you'll see that 80% are new to their positions, and half of those employees are new to PerkinElmer.

How have you managed to bring along existing employees—the "core," as you put it?

We try to make sure all employees have challenging goals, support for professional development, and recognition for their accomplishments. And we've made three major changes to our compensation plan. First, we moved away from an economic-value-added (EVA) model to one that is tied to profit and cash targets. That helped focus all our employees on tangible and easily visible goals, and it simplified the previous system. Second, we raised the amount of individual employee compensation that is determined by performance. Third, we created an employee stock purchase plan and turned our options plan upside down. In the past, some 75% of the options were distributed at the corporate level, and the rest were given out at the business-unit level. The reverse is true today.

We have also put into place a broad range of training programs that touch all of PerkinElmer's 13,000 employees. The activities are designed to teach leadership skills, business fundamentals, and best practices. All of our senior managers, including me, play a role in these programs—either as members of the "faculty" or in give-and-take sessions in which we discuss our progress and disappointments. (See "From Complacency to Competency" at the end of this article.)

Hundreds of books and articles have been written about how to lead change and create a sense of urgency. How do you keep the change message alive for your employees?

Our leadership team reaches out, constantly and directly, to people throughout the organization. I spend a lot of time at "skip level" and town-hall-style meetings with people in each of the businesses. Skip-level meetings bring together a cross section of 15 to 20 employees to talk about what's going well and what we should improve. In an hour or so, I not only develop a better sense of the business, I also have a chance to communicate the values and goals of the company.

I'm also a coach. It's my job to increase the capabilities of leaders throughout the company. As important as recruiting remains, re-recruiting the right people—paying attention to developing people from the inside—is essential. One way we get a picture of the state of our people is through semiannual leadership and organizational reviews of each unit. Each meeting is attended by the unit president and senior managers. We spend a great deal of time evaluating the performance of each of the top 400 people in the company. We come away with a set of priorities about how to improve the business, which might include a list of employees targeted for promotions or developmental moves or a list of targeted new recruits. My personal involvement in the performance reviews of the top 400 people sends a message to everyone that people are critical to PerkinElmer's future.

Strategy and operational decisions are important, but the defining bets are always made on people. If you have the right person leading the charge, good things happen.

Looking back at your first two and a half years at PerkinElmer, were there any surprises?

It's not so much a surprise as it is a confirmation of some great advice I'd been given. Seven years ago, Larry Bossidy [former CEO of AlliedSignal] told me that the most important and memorable decisions are always about people. When I consider the dramatic changes PerkinElmer has already undergone and the group of people who helped make those changes happen, I am even more impressed by the truth of his advice. Strategy and operational decisions are important, but the defining bets are always made on people. If you have the right person leading the charge, whether it's in a factory or a research lab, good things happen. We earned the right to grow, and that's why I see even more opportunities now than when I started this journey.

And Now for Something Completely Different . . .

Selling businesses, improving operations, and acquiring high-growth companies are difficult maneuvers, but attracting the attention of the right outside constituencies is no small task either. Beginning with the company's dramatic name change, Greg Summe describes the challenge of reintroducing PerkinElmer to Wall Street and the rest of the world.

WE DECIDED TO CHANGE our name because we wanted to signal to our customers, investors, and employees that this was a new company. We had already made significant operational, organizational, and portfo-

lio changes, but EG&G's legacy kept dragging us back
to a different era—at least in the minds of Wall Street and
even potential employees. We considered a number of
possibilities, including taking on an entirely new name.
Finally, in 1999, we settled on the PerkinElmer name,
which we had acquired with the instruments business earlier that year, because it already had a prominent product brand with global recognition. We modernized the
PerkinElmer logo and adopted the tag line "precisely" to
communicate the quality of our products and the culture
we wanted to embody. At the time, the name change
was controversial. Many people were emotionally
attached to the old name, and the research we had
done on the impact of a new name was inconclusive. But
today the decision seems like a no-brainer because the
reception has been so positive.

The name change was just part of our journey to
attracting a new group of investors. Historically, EG&G's
stock was held by value-oriented investors, some of
whom had owned EG&G stock since it had gone public
on the New York Stock Exchange in 1965. Many of
them focused chiefly on gains in operating profit and
nominal increases in the price/earnings multiple and
weren't eager to take the risks associated with portfolio
change.

As our earnings and revenue growth accelerated
and our stock price rose, our P/E multiple expanded
beyond the guidelines typically used by value investors.
Therefore, they began to sell their EG&G stock, so we
started reaching out to a new community of Wall Street
analysts and investors. Traditionally, the analysts who
researched and reported on EG&G specialized in industrial, multiproduct companies. But today our research

coverage increasingly comes from analysts who specialize in high-growth markets such as life sciences and telecommunications.

The transition has enabled us to reach a broader base of growth-oriented investors, who support the higher P/E multiple needed to grow our most attractive businesses. Today, 80% of our top 20 investors are growth oriented, compared to 15% early last year.

From Complacency to Competency

PERKINELMER'S TRAINING INITIATIVES, designed to be driven by the developmental needs of individuals, consist of four programs aimed at employees at various levels of the organization.

Advanced Leadership Institute. Designed for middle to senior managers, this three-day program centers on leadership development and business acumen. Through customized computer simulations, participants compete against one another in running PerkinElmer businesses.

Emerging Leaders Program. This three-day program covers business simulations, team projects, best practices, and presentations led by senior managers. It's aimed at early-career managers who have been identified as having high growth potential.

Driving World-Class Performance Program. This two-day course expands on PerkinElmer's core values and processes and teaches the Six Sigma Levels of Performance program, which strives for zero defects in products, services, and transactions. All PerkinElmer employees worldwide will take part in this course; the company's goal is to have every employee trained in Six Sigma by the end of 2001.

Skills-Based Training Programs. These programs are offered on a continuing basis to individual employees. They include training in coaching, team building, project management, and assessment skills.

Originally published in November–December 2000
Reprint R00607

The Tough Work of Turning Around a Team

BILL PARCELLS

Executive Summary

BILL PARCELLS, ONE OF the NFL's winningest coaches, offers business leaders three rules for reversing the fortunes of a losing team. He contends that the keys to motivating people are much the same whether they're playing on a football field or working in an office.

The first rule is to make it clear from day one that you're in charge. Parcells has found that holding frank one-on-one conversations with every member of the organization is essential to success. Leaders can do everything right with their teams and still fail if they aren't able to reach each member as an individual.

Rule two is that confrontation is healthy. Parcells relishes confrontation because it provides an opportunity to get things straight with people. Confrontation does not mean putting someone down. When criticizing members

105

of the team, he puts it in a positive context. One he sets that context, he's not afraid to be blunt about players' failings.

Parcells's third rule is to identify small goals and hit them. He believes that success breeds success. Once a team gets in the habit of losing, confidence dips and success seems unreachable. To break the habit of losing, Parcells focuses on achieving goals within immediate reach.

In the end, Parcells is convinced that if you get people on your team who share the same goals and the same passion, and if you push them to achieve at the highest level, you're going to come out on top.

THE PEOPLE IN YOUR COMPANY have little loyalty; some even want you to fail. Your star performers expect constant pampering. Your stockholders are impatient, demanding quick results. And the media scrutinize and second-guess your every move.

I can relate.

As a coach in the NFL, I've been in a lot of pressure-cooker situations, and my guess is that the challenges I've faced are not all that different from the ones that executives deal with every day. I'm not saying that business is like football. I am saying that people are people, and that the keys to motivating them and getting them to perform to their full potential are pretty much the same whether they're playing on a football field or working in an office.

The toughest challenge I've faced as a coach is taking a team that's performing poorly and turning it around. I've done it three times now. In 1983, my first year as a head coach, I led the New York Giants through an abysmal season—we won only three games. In the next six seasons, we climbed to the top of the league, winning two Super Bowls. When I became coach of the New England Patriots in 1993, they were coming off two years in which they'd won a combined total of three games. In 1996, we were in the Super Bowl. In 1997, when I came to the New York Jets, the team had just suffered through a 1-15 season. Two years later, we made it to the conference championship.

The only way to change people is to tell them in the clearest possible terms what they're doing wrong. And if they don't want to listen, they don't belong on the team.

Those turnarounds taught me a fundamental lesson about leadership: You have to be honest with people— brutally honest. You have to tell them the truth about their performance, you have to tell it to them face-to-face, and you have to tell it to them over and over again. Sometimes the truth will be painful, and sometimes saying it will lead to an uncomfortable confrontation. So be it. The only way to change people is to tell them in the clearest possible terms what they're doing wrong. And if they don't want to listen, they don't belong on the team.

Taking Charge

To lead, you've got to be a leader. That may sound obvious, but it took me an entire year to learn—and it wasn't a pleasant year. When I started as coach of the Giants, I lacked confidence. I was surrounded by star players with big names and big egos, and I was a little tentative in dealing with them. I didn't confront them about how they needed to change to succeed. As a result, I didn't get their respect and I wasn't able to change their attitudes. So they just kept on with their habit of losing.

At the end of the season, I figured I'd be fired. But management ended up asking me back for another season—mainly because they couldn't find anybody to replace me. At that point, I knew I had nothing to lose, so I decided I would do it my way. I was going to lead and the players were going to follow, and that's all there was to it. On the first day of training camp, I laid it on the line: I told everyone that losing would no longer be tolerated. Players who were contributing to the team's weak performance would be given a chance to change, and if they didn't change, they'd be gone.

It was a tough message, but I balanced it with a more positive one. I told them what I think a team is all about: achievement. Sure, they could make a lot of money in football and they could buy a lot of nice things, but the only permanent value of work lies in achievement, and that comes only with relentless effort and commitment. It wasn't going to be easy, but at the end of the day, achievement would be the most important thing they would take home with them.

After I talked to them as a group and established my credibility as a leader, I began talking with them personally. With the Giants, and with the other teams I've coached, I've found that holding frank, one-on-one conversations with every member of the organization is essential to success. It allows me to ask each player for his support in helping the team achieve its goals, and it allows me to explain exactly what I expect from him. I try to appeal to the players' passion for achievement and winning, but I'm also very clear that if they don't give the team what it needs, then I'm going to find someone else who will. I tell them, "If you don't want to play in the championship games and you don't want to achieve at the highest level, then I don't want you here, because that's what I'm trying to do. I am not trying to finish fourth." Leaders can do everything right with their teams and still fail if they don't deliver their message to each member as an individual.

Those conversations also give me a basis for making an honest evaluation of every player. It's all too easy to come into an organization that's been struggling and make blanket judgments about everybody—to think everybody's failing. But that's a mistake. There can be many hidden strengths on a team, just as there can be many hidden weaknesses. The only way you can bring them to the surface is by watching and talking with each team member. You'll quickly see who's a contributor and who's an obstacle. And, for the good of the team, you'll want to move swiftly to get the obstacles out of the way. The hard fact is that some people will never change.

So if you're called in to turn around a team, here's Rule One: make it clear from day one that you're in charge. Don't wait to earn your leadership; impose it.

The Power of Confrontation

If you want to get the most out of people, you have to apply pressure—that's the only thing that any of us really responds to. As a coach, I've always tried to turn up the heat under my people, to constantly push them to perform at a high level.

Creating pressure in an organization requires confrontation, and it can get very intense, very emotional.

I've seen coaches avoid confrontations with their players because they don't like conflict, and I assume the same thing is true among the leaders of business teams. But I've actually come to relish confrontation, not because it makes me feel powerful but because it provides an opportunity to get things straight with people. It's not until you look people right in the eye that you get to the sources of their behavior and motivation. Without confrontation, you're not going to change the way they think and act.

Confrontation does not mean putting someone down. When you criticize members of the team, you need to put it in a positive context. I've often said to a player, "I don't think you're performing up to your potential; you can do better." But I also made it clear that my goals were his goals: "It's in your best interest that you succeed, and it's in my best interest that you succeed. We really want the same thing." Once you set that context, though, you shouldn't be afraid to be blunt about people's failings. You shouldn't be afraid to offend them. You need to do what it takes to get a strong reaction because then you know you've reached them.

Even as I'm confronting players about their weaknesses, I'm also always trying to rebuild a culture of success.

In the end, I've found, people like the direct approach. It's much more valuable to them to have a leader who's absolutely clear and open than to have one who softsoaps or talks in circles. I've had many players come back to me ten years later and thank me for putting the pressure on them. They say what they remember most about me is one line: "I think you're better than you think you are." In fact, they say they use the same line with their kids when they're not doing so well in school or are having other problems. My father used that expression with me, and there's a lot of truth to it—people can do more than they think they can.

That's Rule Two: confrontation is healthy.

Success Breeds Success

The prospect of going from a team that's at the bottom of the standings to one that's on top is daunting. When you've done a lot of losing, it gets hard to imagine yourself winning. So even as I'm confronting players about their weaknesses, I'm also always trying to build a culture of success. That's not something you can do overnight. You have to go one step at a time, the same way you move the ball down the field, yard by yard.

Here's my philosophy: to win games, you need to believe as a team that you have the ability to win games. That is, confidence is born only of demonstrated ability. This may sound like a catch-22, but it's important to remember that even small successes can be extremely powerful in helping people believe in themselves.

In training camp, therefore, we don't focus on the ultimate goal—getting to the Super Bowl. We establish a clear set of goals that are within immediate reach: we're going to be a smart team; we're going to be a well-conditioned team; we're going to be a team that plays hard; we're going to be a team that has pride; we're going to be a team that wants to win collectively; we're going to be a team that doesn't criticize one another.

When we start acting in ways that fulfill these goals, I make sure everybody knows it. I accentuate the positive at every possible opportunity, and at the same time I emphasize the next goal that we need to fulfill. If we have a particularly good practice, then I call the team together and say, "We got something done today; we executed real well. I'm very pleased with your work. But here's what I want to do tomorrow: I want to see flawless special teams work. If you accomplish that, then we'll be ready for the game on Sunday."

When you set small, visible goals, and people achieve them, they start to get it into their heads that they can succeed. They break the habit of losing and begin to get into the habit of winning. It's extremely satisfying to see that kind of shift take place in the way a team thinks about itself.

So Rule Three is: set small goals and hit them.

Picking the Right People

Another challenge in building a winning team comes from free agency. I know that companies today are having trouble hanging on to their best people; there's a great deal of turnover and not much loyalty. That's a situation that I had to adapt to as a coach.

One of the things that initially helped me become successful in the NFL was my ability to develop players with the Giants. We had a program in place, and we brought people along slowly. Today, you no longer have the time to develop your talent in the old way. The situation is more like coaching high school football in some respects— every year, the senior class graduates and moves on. When I started, coaches reworked maybe 8% or 10% of their teams every year. Now it's sometimes as high as 30%.

That kind of turnover adds a tough new wrinkle to turning a team around and keeping it on the winning track. In particular, you have to be extremely careful about the new people you bring on. You can do serious damage with a few bad choices. Unfortunately, there's no science to picking the right people. There's a lot of trial and error involved. You're going to get fooled by people, and you're going to make mistakes—I know I've made my share. But after a while, you start to develop a sense of who's likely to work out. I've found it's not always the one who has the best reputation or even the most outstanding set of talents. It's usually the one who understands what it will take to succeed and is committed to making the effort.

For example, there's a player, Bryan Cox, who had a terrible reputation in the NFL. He'd been fined a lot of money by the league—maybe more than anyone in its history. My teams had played against him so many times that I almost felt like I knew him. And watching him play, I'd say to myself, this guy plays so hard and tries so hard—he's got something that I want to have on my team. So when he was a free agent, I called him on the phone and we had a straight, tough talk. I told him exactly what I wanted from him, and he told me what he wanted from me, which boiled down to this: "Don't BS me." I told him he'd always know what I was thinking. Bryan signed on with the Jets, and he's done a great job for the franchise.

I'm no psychologist. I don't care about what kind of personality someone has or whether it corresponds with my own. I don't care if they're "well adjusted." I just want my players to want to win as much as I want to win. I'm convinced that if you get people onto your team who share the same goals and the same passion, and if you push them to achieve at the highest level, you're going to come out on top.

Originally published in November–December 2000
Reprint R00613

Saving Money, Saving Lives

JON MELIONES

Executive Summary

IN 1996, DUKE CHILDREN'S HOSPITAL was in serious trouble. Its $11 million annual operating loss had forced administrators to make cutbacks. As a result, some caregivers felt that the quality of care had deteriorated. Parents' complaints were on the rise. Frustrated staff members were quitting.

In this article, Jon Meliones, DCH's chief medical director, candidly describes how his debt-ridden hospital transformed itself into a vibrant and profitable one. The problem, he realized, was that each group in DCH was focusing only on its individual mission. Doctors and nurses wanted to restore their patients to health; they didn't want to have to think about costs. Hospital administrators, for their part, were focused only on controlling widely escalating health care costs. To keep DCH afloat, clinicians and administrators needed to work together.

By listening to staff concerns, turning reams of confusing data into useful information, taking a fresh approach to teamwork, and using the balanced scorecard method, Meliones and his colleagues brought DCH back to life. Developing and implementing the balanced scorecard approach wasn't easy: it took a pilot project, a top-down reorganization, development of a customized information system, and systematic work redesign. But their efforts paid off. Customer satisfaction ratings jumped 18%. Improvements to internal business processes reduced the average length of stay 21% while the readmission rate fell from 7% to 3%. The cost per patient dropped nearly $5,000. And DCH recorded profits of $4 million in 2000.

This first-person account is required reading for any executive seeking to revitalize a sagging organization. Meliones shares the operating principles DCH followed to become a thriving business.

My EPIPHANY CAME AT seven o'clock on a hectic November evening in 1996. I was the attending physician in the intensive care unit at Duke Children's Hospital (DCH) in Durham, North Carolina. A six-month-old named Alex lay in a crib in the ICU with a stiff plastic tube in her throat. Awake and moving after heart surgery, the tiny girl was ready to come off the ventilator. As Alex squirmed and tried to breathe, the ventilator forced more air into her lungs. Her exhausted parents grew distraught. "Why can't she come off the ventilator?" her mother asked. "Because we've had to cut back on night staff," replied the busy nurse. "There's no respiratory therapist available." Alex was uncomfortable. She received medication to help her sleep and to keep her from fighting the ventilator until the therapist arrived in the morning. But her parents didn't sleep; they were too confused and upset.

As I watched Alex and her parents, I thought back to similar scenes I had witnessed over the years at DCH, a 134-bed pediatric hospital located on the fifth floor of Duke University Hospital. Here, 800 employees care for patients in our neonatal intensive care unit, pediatric intensive care unit and pediatric emergency room, bone-marrow transplant and intermediate care units, as well as in our subspecialty and outreach clinics. When I came to DCH in 1992, we had a $4 million annual operating loss; it had grown to $11 million by 1996, which forced administrators to cut back on resources. As a result, some caregivers felt that the quality of clinical care had deteriorated. Parents' complaints increased. Some dissatisfied doctors threatened to send their patients elsewhere. Frustrated staff quit.

And then it struck me. I saw with perfect clarity the reason that DCH was struggling to meet the needs of its customers—our patients and their parents. And I knew what had to be done to make things right. The problem was that our hospital was a collection of fiefdoms: each group, from accountants to administrators to clinicians, was focusing on its individual goal rather than on the organization as a whole. We would be a far more effective organization if we could stop that from happening. Most companies in the United States had this insight 20 years ago, but the nonprofit world remains, for the most part, unaware of it. I realized that DCH needed to start thinking less like a money-losing nonprofit and more like a profitable corporation.

A sense of mission, of course, is critical to any organization's identity. The institutional mission of a hospital is to promote the health of the community. But during difficult periods, it's easy to lose sight of the big picture and focus solely on your fiefdom's specific goals. Clinicians—that is, doctors and nurses—want to restore their patients to health; they don't want to think about costs. Hospital administrators have their own mission—to control wildly escalating health care costs.

Cost cutting in a vacuum traumatizes patients, frustrates clinicians, and ultimately cripples the hospital's mission. The decision to cut a respiratory therapist from the night shift, for example, affected Alex and her parents as well as their insurance company, which had to pay an additional $2,000 to cover the cost of the ventilator and ICU care. The decision also left the clinicians feeling powerless, since decisions regarding clinical practice were being made without their input. Such trade-offs between quality of patient care and cost control cause intense conflict for health care professionals. In worst-case situations, efforts to improve profit margins actually have the opposite effect—they chase away customers, cost executives their jobs, and put the entire hospital at risk of financial ruin.

Regaining Our Balance

Considering the magnitude of the issues we faced—a $7 million increase in annual losses in four years—it's hard to believe that we ever turned things around. But we did, by changing people's minds and hearts, inch by inch, day by day. In 1997, the chief nurse executive, nurse managers, and I began working together to start turning the organization around. First, we discussed our current realities with the entire clinical team. We opened the meetings by talking about our goals for our patients. "We want patients to be happy," the doctors and nurses agreed, "and for them to have the best care." We also described our pressing financial challenges.

We showed the clinicians our raw data. The average length of stay at DCH was eight days—20% longer than the six-day national average. The average per-patient cost was $15,000—more money than we were bringing in. If we continued to spend at the same rates, we would be forced to cut clinical programs, staff, and beds. The quality of patient care and our reputation would then suffer, and we would fail to meet the needs of our community.

Confronted with this grim picture, the clinicians began to understand that if we wanted to save our programs and our patients, create an environment in which staff are fulfilled, and keep our jobs, we would all have to readjust our individual missions and start paying attention to costs. If the hospital didn't show a margin, clinicians wouldn't be able to fulfill their mission. Thus, we adopted the now-familiar mantra in health care: no margin, no mission.

It was also clear that the administrators needed to be highly involved. To bring the administrators' and the clinicians' missions into alignment, we turned to a practical management approach that had worked well in numerous *Fortune* 500 corporations: the balanced scorecard method. Developed by Robert Kaplan and David Norton, it had improved customer service, driven organizational change, and boosted bottom-line performance in leading companies like AT&T, Intel, and 3M. Our goal was to become the health care leader in the balanced scorecard. (See "A Look at the Numbers" for DCH's results.)

Our balanced scorecard aligned the hospital's goals along four equally important quadrants: financial health;

A Look at the Numbers

Using the balanced scorecard method, Duke Children's Hospital's cost-per-case average fell from nearly $15,000 to $10,500 and its margin soared from an $11 million annual loss to a $4 million gain.

Cost per case

$14,889

$13,411

$12,550 $12,440

$10,500

1996   1997   1998   1999   2000

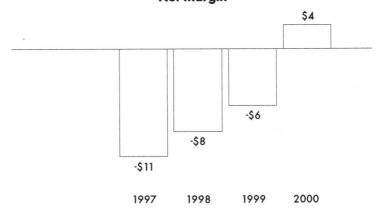

Net margin

$4

-$6

-$8

-$11

1997   1998   1999   2000

customer satisfaction; internal business procedures; and employee satisfaction. We explained the theory to clinicians and administrators like this: if you sacrifice too much in one quadrant to satisfy another, your organization as a whole is thrown out of balance. We could, for example, cut costs to improve the financial quadrant by firing half the staff, but that would hurt quality of service, and the customer quadrant would fall out of balance. Or we could increase productivity in the internal business quadrant by assigning more patients to a nurse, but doing so would raise the likelihood of errors—an unacceptable trade-off. Our vision, which became the new mission statement, was to provide patients and families with high quality, compassionate care within an efficient organization.

Taking Our Medicine

Developing and implementing a balanced scorecard is labor intensive because it is a consensus-driven methodology. To make ours work required nothing short of a pilot project, a top-down reorganization, development of a customized information system, and systematic work redesign. The most difficult challenge was convincing employees that they must work in different ways.

At first, doctors and managers saw attempts to move them into teams as a shift in their power base. Nearly everyone complained that applying a systematic approach to cost management was "cookbook medicine." It took a good deal of persuasion, persistence, and reassurance to get some individuals to buy into our process. One cardiologist routinely stormed out of meetings when we talked about cost per case.

We knew that changing people's minds would be hard work. But once people saw how successful the balanced scorecard approach was in one area of the hospital, we reasoned, it would be easier to sell the methodology throughout the rest of the organization. So we decided to launch a pilot project. Some physicians were much more willing to change than others. Those who understood the importance of applying systems to medicine—such as surgeons—became our first champions. So we started the balanced scorecard in one very important microcosm of the hospital—the pediatric intensive care unit, which I lead.

First, we reorganized the roles that individuals play in the ICU. We moved from mission-bound departments in which people identified only with their particular jobs ("I am a manager," "I am a nurse," and so on) to goal-oriented, multidisciplinary teams focused on a particular illness or disease ("We, the ICU team, consisting of the manager, the nurse, the physician, the pharmacist, and the radiologist, help children with heart problems"). We called these teams clinical business units—what other industries call business or operating units. The lead physician and the lead administrator shared responsibility in these teams. Together, they reviewed financial information, patient and staff satisfaction data, and information on health care trends and initiatives.

The various clinical business units worked together to organize "care coordination rounds" and brainstorm solutions to difficult patient cases. They created a patient's care plan—a document, shared with the parents, that records everything from treatment recommendations to post-hospital care.

The teams also developed protocols we call clinical pathways—a set of best practices for various treatments. For example, a respiratory therapist, a nurse, and a physician developed a series of steps a nurse could follow to remove a patient from a respirator without having a therapist present. As the clinicians developed new pathways, they shared their successes with the entire organization so we could all learn from their experience.

By developing and promoting protocols like these, we improved care dramatically. For example, we knew that babies recovering from heart surgery had trouble feeding and that parents needed to learn how to help them. Before we had formed the pathways, we would wait until the day of discharge to teach parents how to do so. Once people started sharing their expertise to develop the pathways, we learned that there was no reason to wait so long and moved the training to the day after surgery. Patients were able to go home much sooner, and their hospital costs were cut by 28%.

Within six months, our balanced scorecard approach reduced the cost per case in the ICU by nearly 12% and improved our patient satisfaction by 8%.

We developed more protocols by comparing patient data. A study of 20 heart patients, for example, revealed that treatment costs varied dramatically. One child received two days' worth of antibiotics; another received seven days' worth for the same condition. One child underwent ten laboratory tests; another had only three, and so on. As a group, the clinicians went over each case, comparing notes and reviewing the medical literature. They decided which tests were unnecessary and eliminated them.

Within six months, our balanced scorecard approach in the ICU was garnering impressive results. We reduced the cost per case by nearly 12% and improved our measured patient satisfaction by 8%. In fact, our pilot project was working so well that we implemented it in pediatrics, then in all of the other areas of DCH, within a year. We didn't use a cookie-cutter approach; rather, leaders in each unit customized the scorecard template for their specific areas.

Over time, even the physician who had angrily left our initial meetings began to find ways to lower his cost per case without compromising patient care. For example, instead of keeping some patients awaiting surgery in the hospital, he discharged them overnight to a nearby hotel, lowering the total cost by $1,000 per day while making the patients and their parents much more comfortable.

A Measure of Progress

Like most hospitals, DCH collects a tremendous amount of data. We rigorously detail things like length of stay, number of staff, cost per case, and so on. But we were culling very little useful information from the data—and some of it was false. For example, the first report card on my own performance showed that I had discharged 70 patients with an average length of stay of 29 days and an average cost per case of $70,000. Taken together, these numbers deserved a grade of F. I knew that since I'd been head of the intensive care unit, I'd cared for and transferred 1,500 patients. What was going on here? A closer look at the data revealed that they reported on only the 70 patients who had died, not my total caseload.

Clearly, we needed to approach the data in a new way and turn it into useful information. Unless we did, we wouldn't know where our potential cost savings were. We didn't know, for example, that babies were needlessly kept on $2,000 ventilators at night, nor did we know how much that decision was costing the hospital. So for every clinical business unit, we created a measurement system for each of the four balanced scorecard quadrants.

To measure our progress, we asked our IT department to help us develop our own database and cost-accounting system. Using information pulled from national databases, we determined national averages for indicators such as length of stay and complication rates. (In 1997, custom development was our only option. We've since installed StrategicVision software from SAS to support our extensive data management, trend analysis, and performance reporting needs.) The system logged each patient's treatment history and costs for everything from a $15 hypodermic needle to a $5,000 heart-lung bypass operation. The system also tracked the average waiting times for admission and discharge, blood culture contamination rates, and so on.

The new system helped us find ways to improve our performance in each of the four quadrants. Many of the steps we took were small, but cumulatively, they made a big difference. For example, our clinical pathways included a "patient care guide" for parents that explained in lay terms what they could expect to happen on a daily basis during their child's hospital stay. We also learned from our customer surveys that parents felt frustrated by not knowing who their child's attending physician or nurse was at any given time. So we simply put identification cards on the doors, naming the attending doctor and primary nurse. Our customer satisfaction scores rose sharply.

We made other changes, too. For the financial quadrant, for example, we reviewed the most significant data points, such as the number of patients admitted, treated, and released, and the cost per patient. The clinical business units reviewed cases of patients whose diagnostic,

surgical, pharmacy, and postoperation costs had been
the highest, and tried to determine why. In many cases,
our research showed us new ways to do business. For
example, we learned that children often stayed longer
than necessary in our $1,700-per-day ICU, in which the
nurse to patient ratio is 1 to 1 or 1 to 2. That was because
the patients weren't quite
ready to move to the regu-
lar pediatric floor, where
the ratio of nurses to
patients is 1 to 5 and the
cost is $700 per day. So we
created a six-bed, $1,200-
per-day transitional care unit, where the nurse to patient
ratio is 1 to 3. Patients could stay there until they could
be moved to the general floor. Not only did our cost-
per-patient numbers drop but also our patients' families
got to spend more time with their recovering children.

*The cost per patient
dropped by nearly $5,000—
a fact not lost on parents,
insurers, and our own
senior leaders.*

Overall, the results we've achieved at DCH by using
the balanced scorecard have been stunning. By increasing the number of clinical pathways and communicating
more with parents, our customer satisfaction ratings
jumped by 18%. Improvements to our internal business
processes reduced the average length of stay from 7.9
days in 1996 to 6.1 days in fiscal year 2000, while the
readmission rate fell from 7% to 3%. And employees
noted a 45% increase in satisfaction with children's services and with the way the entire administrative team
performed its job.

Impressive results occurred on the financial front,
too. The cost per patient dropped by nearly $5,000—a
fact not lost on parents, insurers, and our own senior
leaders. By FY 2000, we had gone from $11 million in

losses to profits of $4 million, even though we were admitting more patients. We achieved a reduction in costs of $29 million over these four years, without staff cutbacks. Our methodology has proved so successful that the entire Duke University Hospital now uses it as a framework. With the balanced scorecard we have drastically improved our margin and achieved our hospital's mission. (For more on how to turn your organization around, see "Survival Strategies" at the end of this article.)

Lessons Learned

Yes, DCH has navigated a tremendous turnaround, but I don't want to suggest that it's been easy. Adopting the balanced scorecard approach presented us with huge management challenges on a daily basis. In the early stages, we often found it difficult to keep discussions on target. We spent nearly a month debating whether a certain goal or target belonged in the internal business process quadrant or the customer satisfaction quadrant. We learned to limit those discussions—it was too easy to get embroiled in semantics and lose our focus on patients and staff.

There's a fine art to communicating with professionals who know more than you do about their particular subject and who are passionate about their work.

We also found that people became demoralized if we compared their performance to an abstract or too-lofty target. For that reason, we encouraged employees to use their own performance as the primary benchmark. Still, if they wanted to see how their performance compared with the hospital as a whole, or with a national average, they could review those data points as well.

We learned to set our targets conservatively at first: an annual 10% reduction in the length of stay was something most of us felt comfortable reaching for, but a goal of 20% would have been too intimidating. As we became more successful, we set more aggressive targets.

And I learned that there's a fine art to communicating with professionals who know more than you do about their particular subject and who are passionate about their work. You can't just order them around. You have to get inside their heads and figure out what they're going through.

Before 1996, I thought I was a decent communicator. But over time, I've had to learn to listen carefully not only to what people are telling me but also to what I'm saying to them. Today I know that I can't make a point in a conversation by talking in the abstract. I have to say something that personally matters to the other individual. I learned not to say things like, "Duke Children's Hospital is losing $11 million per year." Rather, I opened conversations with a question, such as "How important do you think it is to have a therapist on this unit to work with your patients?" When they said it was important, I'd follow up with "How can we work together to manage our costs so we can preserve the therapist's job?"

I learned that little things make a big difference when it comes to morale building. We created all kinds of communication and feedback mechanisms. I started a newsletter, "Practicing Smarter," so staff members could share best practices and keep one another apprised of their progress. We honored "team members of the month," started on-line discussion groups, and sponsored a series of staff brown-bag lunches and open forums. These approaches may sound simple, but they really did help to change our culture. For the first time, employees felt that their opinions mattered.

I discovered how important it is to share the pulpit during dramatic organizational changes. Not only did I respect the chief nurse executive, the managers, and the administrators as partners, but I knew that they could communicate more effectively with their own constituencies than I ever could.

Even in the most earnest conversations, I've found that having a sense of humor is essential. For example, I developed a Letterman-style list of the "Top Ten Reasons for Using the Balanced Scorecard," poking fun at myself in meetings. Once, I even walked through the hospital dressed up as the eminently poke-able Pillsbury Doughboy. Keeping things light made it easier for us all to endure the tremendously challenging course we'd set for ourselves.

I learned, too, to respect the persuasive power of meaningful information. I spent hours with members of our IT department, telling them what the staff was telling me—trying to slice and dice our enormous mountains of data into useful information. When we finally presented people with accurate tracking measures about their personal performance, they were fascinated—and anxious to improve.

It's been four years since we set out to improve performance at Duke Children's Hospital, and changes are still happening. We talk about our scorecard constantly; we're fine-tuning what works and discarding what doesn't. Whenever a clinician comes up with a better pathway, we spread the word through our newsletter and on our bulletin boards.

Of all the changes that have occurred, the most telling are the ones we see in our patients. Consider the case of Ryan, a four-month-old who recently recovered from heart surgery. At 8 P.M., Ryan was breathing with a ventilator—just as Alex had—and his parents kept vigil by his crib. But unlike Alex's parents, Ryan's parents knew exactly who was responsible for their child's care, what his care entailed, and that he'd soon be transferred to an intermediate care unit. At 9 P.M., Ryan began breathing on his own. The nurse skillfully removed the plastic tube and gently placed him on his mother's lap. For me, seeing Ryan sleeping peacefully in his mother's arms was a rewarding end to a long, hard, but ultimately satisfying journey.

Survival Strategies

The challenges faced by Duke Children's Hospital are by no means unique to the health care industry. Indeed, many organizations find themselves in similar situations. They fear that focusing on costs will compromise their higher mission of serving the community—but in fact, a strong bottom line will make fulfilling their missions that much easier. If you're trying to turn your organization around, you may want to adopt the operating principles we followed to make DCH a thriving business.

Communicate, Communicate, Communicate

- If your organization is in trouble, be honest. Make it absolutely clear to everyone in the company that survival depends on cost management.

- Listen to what employees are saying; they know their jobs better than you do. Instead of issuing orders, ask them, "What can we (as an organization) do?"
- Share the pulpit. People with other expertise can help build consensus.
- Change people's roles; instead of identifying with an individual job ("I am a nurse"), employees should identify with goal-oriented teams ("We, the ICU team, work together to help children with heart problems").
- Offer constant feedback. Frequent evaluations help keep the organization on track.
- Publicly celebrate every employee and team success.
- Cultivate your sense of humor—people will respond if you can laugh at yourself.

Chart Your Path

- Start with a pilot project; succeeding in one department will pave the way for organizationwide change.
- Set conservative goals at first; you'll gain the confidence needed to set more aggressive targets.
- Focus on a few key goals; changing everything at once leads to failure.
- Turn data into information. Work with your information technology people to ensure that employees can correctly interpret measurements and statistics.
- Let employees compete with their own performance, not with some abstract competitive or statistical target.

Never Stop

- When mapping your business to the balanced scorecard, don't get sidetracked by semantics.

- Be willing to experiment; learn from failures.
- Constantly revise and improve practices.
- Encourage strategic thinking at all levels.

Originally published in November–December 2000
Reprint R00612

Harley's Leadership U-Turn

RICH TEERLINK

Executive Summary

WHEN RICH TEERLINK, now retired chairman and CEO of Harley-Davidson, became president and COO of its motorcycle division in 1987, the hard work of saving the company was already done. The company had just survived seven arduous years of crisis and was on a steady path toward growth.

Realizing how much circumstances had changed, Teerlink immediately saw the need for a new kind of leadership—one far removed from the command-and-control model that had carried it throughout its turnaround. What the company needed instead was leadership that would encourage employees to break new ground—an environment where both union and salaried employees would want to do better, where they'd care about the company on a personal level and work together to improve both individual and overall performance.

In this First Person account, Teerlink tells the story of how difficult it was to make that shift. Even if you are hardwired (like he is) to share power rather than exert it, he says, it's extremely hard to avoid the top-down approach. In a plan to improve operations, for example, Teerlink came up with an idea for a program he hoped would motivate every employee, customer, and stakeholder. The program, called gain sharing, would allow every employee to share in the company's financial success. The problem? As his then consultant Lee Ozley pointed out, the program was yet another initiative created and imposed from the top.

Throughout his tenure, Rich Teerlink launched several programs designed to elicit ideas, enthusiasm, concerns, and vision from employees. These initiatives—as well as other efforts toward inclusiveness—have helped transform Harley's culture and made it the success story it is today.

W HEN I BECAME PRESIDENT and COO of Harley-Davidson's motorcycle division in 1987, the hard work of saving the company was done. We had survived seven arduous years of crisis. But that hardly meant Easy Street lay ahead. In fact, we faced an altogether new and daunting challenge—sustaining progress. But how to do that? For me, the answer was clear—especially when it came to issues of leadership. We needed to create an environment at Harley where *everyone* took responsibility for the company's present and its future.

I knew that such an approach wouldn't come naturally to Harley. After all, our crisis had been managed with an unmistakable top-down approach, as is so often the case with turnarounds. But now that times had changed, so, too, could our way of doing things. I believed then, and still do, that people are an organization's only sustainable competitive advantage. The leader should mind the interests of all stakeholders, of course, but he or she should also be an outspoken advocate for employees, making sure they are front and center in an organization.

It's important for people to understand that even if you are hardwired, like me, to be a leader who shares power rather than exerts it—even if you set out to be a listener and a team player—the command-and-control model is hard to avoid. That's because the top management job carries certain expectations on behalf of employees, colleagues, and the outside world. It takes trust on the part of employees and discipline on the part of the leader to push back on those traditional expectations and create a company where decisions and accountability are owned by all.

Even if you are hardwired to be a leader who shares power rather than exerts it, the command-and-control model is hard to avoid.

Survival Mode

My career with Harley-Davidson dates back to August 1981 when I joined as CFO. I began my new job just two months after a group of 13 Harley managers had bought the company from its then parent company, AMF, in a leveraged buyout. I knew I was walking into a tough situation. Harley-Davidson was certainly an American icon, but back then it wasn't having any success in the marketplace. It had a poor reputation for quality and reliability, and it was behind the curve on product design and development. Break-even points were high and, not surprisingly, market share was falling. What's more, the company faced some of the toughest competitors in the world: Honda and Yamaha. It's no wonder that in 1980, when AMF engaged an investment bank to sell the division, it found no takers.

When an organization is under extreme pressure—so much so that one wrong move can mean its collapse—authoritarian leadership may very well be necessary. It certainly allows managers to act fast. Vaughn Beals needed speed, and so that's the kind of leadership style he tended to use. Indeed, it came to him quite naturally.

Over the next few years, Vaughn and the leadership team (of which I was member) cut the overall workforce by 40%—affecting both the salaried ranks and the hourly workforce. All remaining salaried employees took a 9% pay cut and agreed to have their pay frozen at those reduced levels for at least two years. This change, and many others, originated at the top of the corporate pyramid, with no room for push back from the ranks below.

By the mid-1980s, it appeared that Vaughn and the team might pull off the miracle Harley needed. The company had introduced its Evolution Engine in 1984, and that engine, combined with the new Softail product line (an elegant variation on the classic Harley look), began to make some money. Harley had also initiated special programs to help its dealers attract and retain customers, with notable success. Perhaps the most significant program was—and continues to be—the Harley Owners Group (HOG), created in 1983. Begun as a way to communicate more effectively with the company's end users, HOG quickly grew into the world's largest motorcycle club. And dealers regained confidence that Harley could and would be a dependable partner. At the same time, important improvements were made on the operating side of the business, and a financial restructuring positioned the company to go public.

By 1986, the company's prognosis looked good. Our manufacturing costs were falling; reductions in in-process inventories and associated carrying costs generated savings of more than $40 million a year. Our quality had improved; the number of warranty claims was going down. Our dealer network was revitalized and growing. And then we went public in July, and the offering raised $25 million more than the underwriters had expected.

Engines of Change

Once it was clear the present was in good order, it was time to think about the future. We still had a great deal of rebuilding to do. Yes, we had a great brand, new products were coming to market, quality was improving, and we were making a profit. But our quality standards were not on par with our competitors', and our cost structure was still the highest in the industry. Internally, the company was still a shell of its former self. Whole departments had been hollowed out by the layoffs. And many other good people had left voluntarily, hoping to find more promising futures elsewhere. Who could blame them?

I myself didn't have a plan for the company in my back pocket. I only knew that capturing the ideas of our people—all the people at Harley—was critical to our future success.

Tom Gelb, then vice president of manufacturing, John Campbell, vice president of human resources, and I were meeting a lot in those days—mostly informally—to talk about what the company was doing and why. I knew we

needed big changes in the motorcycle division. We had to
identify some sort of strategy that could carry everyone
forward—everyone meaning employees, customers, and
all other stakeholders. We had to improve operations.
And I felt strongly that we needed to change the way
employees were being treated. They could no longer be
privates, taking orders and operating within strict limits.
We needed to continue to push, and push hard, to create a
much more inclusive and collegial work atmosphere.

One idea we came up with in those meetings was gain
sharing—a program that would allow all employees to
share in the company's financial success. We saw it as a
possible toehold—a way to focus everyone on how we
could all get better together. But an organizational-
change consultant quickly set us straight. He told us that
gain sharing would be like putting a Band-Aid on a gun-
shot wound. He recommended that we talk to a few other
consultants, get their input, and then make the call.

Enter Lee Ozley—the second consultant we spoke
with, the one we hired, the one who has been with the
company ever since, and who has become, over the years,
my mentor, coach, sounding board, and good friend.
Lee's first meeting with me was typical of the kind of
brutal candor he brought to Harley. The gain-sharing
program, he pointed out, had been created at the top and
was about to be imposed from the top. So much for
inclusive leadership!

Good Intentions

Well, we didn't pursue the gain-sharing program.
Instead, over the course of the next several months, we
explored several questions: How does constant crisis
management affect a workforce? How can we—in the
absence of a crisis—create an environment where

employees want to do better, where they care about the company on a personal level and work together to improve both individual and overall performance?

Lee talked a lot about the psychologist Abraham Maslow in those early months. One of Maslow's theories, as many people know, was that absent a crisis, people rarely commit to a program that is imposed on them. But they will willingly commit to a program they help create. That thought made a huge impression on me. And eventually, in late 1988, we agreed to launch a series of programs designed to elicit ideas, thoughts, concerns, complaints, and vision from our employees—across all departments and functions.

First we approached the union leadership of the roughly 700 employees in the Wisconsin operations and asked them to help us create a vision for the business. Lee had warned us that it would take 12 to 18 months to prepare people—both union and salaried leadership—for such a process. But I decided we couldn't wait. Our union contracts expired in three months, and I wanted a new labor-management relationship sanctioned before then. The solution I came up with was to put in place one-year contracts with each local union that included the joint vision-building process. That happened.

Over the next several months, many people in the Wisconsin operations worked hard to craft a joint vision. First, about 70 leaders, both union and management, wrote down their individual ideas for what Harley should become. Then a facilitator met with them in groups to build consensus. Finally, all 70 people met for three days to forge a shared strategic vision for Harley-Davidson. The sense of exhilaration at the end of the process was wonderful.

Our next step was to roll the vision out to the rest of the company. But an interesting thing happened at the first presentation, where union and management leaders were addressing a primarily salaried audience. One of the salaried employees asked, "Who represented us in this process?" I was genuinely ashamed. Once again, we had behaved like traditional managers. We had not included everyone who should have been a part of the process. But we quickly made amends, establishing two groups of salaried employees to share in the responsibility of implementing the vision.

Despite the great progress we made in crafting a shared vision, Lee's warning came home to roost. Our leaders weren't prepared to implement the kind of dramatic change the shared vision called for. In fact, implementing the vision came off as a sort of forced march, sending mixed messages and causing confusion on both the shop floor and in the offices. Not surprisingly, the largest local union opted out of the process after two years. I learned that changing people's long-held assumptions and behaviors takes time. That doesn't mean you give up; it just means you keep your focus and accept that the journey has its downs as well as its ups. Ultimately, although the joint visioning process did not succeed as we had hoped, it did lay the groundwork for shared leadership agreements with the unions in 1997.

What Does Rich Want?

In March 1989, I became CEO, and I soon decided that it was time to bring together the company's 60 senior executives at an off-site meeting. I wanted them to get to know one another and begin to work as a truly unified team.

I discussed the idea with Lee and the executive committee, and we developed a program that would feature

two expert speakers on the issue of change and one outside CEO who had led a major change effort. After hear-
ing the presentations, we would break into groups and
talk about what we'd heard, what we thought we could
accomplish, and how we could do it.

At the opening ceremony, I addressed the group.
"We're here to learn," I said. "There are no right answers.
We're here to have fun,
to get to know one
another." And indeed,
that's what seemed to
happen—at first. The
speakers were well
received, and the first
night, people did skits that were hilarious—the ice
seemed to have been broken. I was feeling good about
the whole event.

*I noticed, as I went into each
room, the question "What
does Rich want?" on many of
the easels the groups were
using to record their thoughts.*

As planned, after each speaker, we moved into smaller
cross-divisional, divisional, functional, and cross-functional groups. People in these groups would talk, and as
they did, I would visit each cluster with the speaker so
that people could ask questions. I noticed, as I went into
each room, the question "What does Rich want?" on
many of the easels the groups were using to record their
thoughts.

I felt terrible. I thought we had been so clear at the
outset that the point was not to figure out what I wanted
but to figure out what everyone wanted for the company.
The senior executives weren't supposed to be trying to
guess the right answer according to Rich. And yet,
clearly, they had a concern about a hidden agenda.

At the closing session, I expressed my frustration. I
blasted the whole group. I said, "We need a revolution,
and I'm not going to lead it. You need to lead it." I told

them I was disappointed with what I'd seen on the easels. That ended the meeting.

When I returned to the office on Monday, one of my colleagues was waiting for me. She took me aside and let me have it. She said, "You know, you really stuck a pin in our balloon at that session. We were doing fine. We were going through a natural process, getting to know one another, expressing our fears as well as our thoughts about what we wanted for the company."

And then I realized that what had been upsetting me most was simply that the participants had not done what I wanted them to do. My ego got in the way. Rather than being happy that people were talking, and understanding that it was normal for people to want to figure out whether "the boss" had an agenda, I had, in my heated enthusiasm for inclusivity, picked up on—and picked at—what was in reality a minor point. My expectations weren't important at that exercise. What was important were their expectations. And they were happy. Too frequently, we as leaders are trying to satisfy ourselves rather than others.

Fortunately, that colleague felt comfortable enough to tell me that I had been wrong. Lee and I talked through the event and discussed why we both felt responsible. We realized, however, we had introduced something that would be useful in the future. And I realized that I had to get myself recalibrated if these meetings

When you're a CEO, there is always a barrier between you and the rest of the company, no matter how hard you try to break it down.

were going to be successful. I did. The second session went well. By the third, we had jettisoned our facilitators—as had been the plan—and took responsibility to teach one another instead of listening to the experts.

Ongoing Process

I retired as Harley's CEO in 1999, and I now serve on its board. Looking back, I can see that many times during the course of my tenure, I slipped in my commitment to inclusive leadership—even as I was preaching its virtues. Each time (or most times—I imagine that there were times when no one called me on it; I hope there weren't too many) Lee or another colleague pulled me up short and reminded me that I wasn't "walking the talk." I was always grateful.

When you're a CEO, there is always a barrier between you and the rest of the company, no matter how hard you try to break it down. And so I also tried very hard to learn to discipline myself—to step out of myself before I spoke or took action and ensure that I wasn't going to slip out of my chosen role.

Overall, I believe I succeeded in my journey to be a different kind of leader. Harley's culture has changed, but the work is not done. Transforming a culture takes time. Everybody hasn't fully bought in to the inclusive approach. We still have some people who think they know all the answers, but these people are getting fewer in number. We still have people who just want to bring their bodies and not their whole selves, mind included, to work. But their ranks are dwindling, too. We've been transforming ourselves since the buyout and will still be at it ten years from now. It is a journey that will never end unless we let it.

Originally published in July–August 2000
Reprint R00411

Waking Up IBM

How a Gang of Unlikely Rebels Transformed Big Blue

GARY HAMEL

Executive Summary

IN THE EARLY 1990s, IBM was a has-been. Fujitsu, Digital Equipment, and Compaq were hammering down its hardware margins. EDS and Andersen Consulting were stealing the hearts of CIOs. Intel and Microsoft were running away with PC profits.

Today, Big Blue is back on top, a leader in e-business services. This is the story of how the company, which had lagged behind every computer trend since the mainframe, caught the Internet wave. Much of the credit for the turnaround goes to a small band of activists who built a bonfire under IBM's rather broad behind.

It stared in February 1994, when a lone midlevel IBM programmer watched Sun Microsystems pirate IBM's Winter Olympics data for its own rogue Web site. Dave Grossman knew that IBM's muckety-mucks were clueless about the Web. But he was convinced that if nothing changed Sun would eat Big Blue's lunch.

Frustrated in his attempts to warn executives over the phone, he drove down to Armonk, walked straight into headquarters with a Unix workstation in his arms, set it up in a closet, and demonstrated the future of computing to a trio of IBM execs. One of them was John Patrick, head of marketing for the hugely successful ThinkPad, who quickly became his mentor. Together, building simultaneously from the top and the bottom of the organization through an ever-widening grassroots coalition of technicians and executives, they put IBM on the Web and morphed it into an e-business powerhouse. People who want to foment similarly successful insurrections can learn a lot from their example.

Do you remember when IBM was a case study in complacency? Insulated from the real world by layer upon layer of dutiful managers and obsequious staff, IBM's executives were too busy fighting their endless turf battles to notice that the company's once unassailable leadership position was crumbling around them. The company that held the top spot on *Fortune*'s list of most admired corporations for four years running in the mid-1980s was in dire need of saving by the early 1990s. Fujitsu, Digital Equipment, and Compaq were hammering down hardware margins. EDS and

How did a company that had lagged behind every computer trend since the mainframe catch the Internet wave—a wave that even Bill Gates and Microsoft originally missed?

Andersen Consulting were stealing the hearts of CIOs.
Intel and Microsoft were running away with PC profits.
Customers were bemoaning the company's arrogance. By
the end of 1994, Lou Gerstner's first full year as CEO, the
company had racked up $15 billion in cumulative losses
over the previous three years, and its market cap had
plummeted from a high of $105 billion to $32 billion.
Armchair consultants were nearly unanimous in their
view: Big Blue should be broken up.

Despite Gerstner's early assertion that IBM didn't
need a strategy (the last thing he wanted was to start
another corporatewide talk fest), IBM was rudderless in
gale force winds. Yet over the next six years, the company transformed itself from a besieged box maker to a
dominant service provider. Its Global Services unit, once
a backwater, grew into a $30 billion business with more
than 135,000 employees, and corporations flocked to
IBM consultants for help in capitalizing on the Internet.
By the end of 1998, IBM had completed 18,000 e-business
consulting engagements, and about a quarter of its $82
billion in revenues was Net related.

How did a company that had lagged behind every
computer trend since the mainframe catch the Internet
wave—a wave that even Bill Gates and Microsoft originally missed? Much of the credit goes to a small band of
activists who built a bonfire under IBM's rather broad
behind. This is their story.

Missing an Olympic Opportunity

The first match was struck in 1994 in the backwoods of
IBM's empire, on a hilltop in Ithaca, New York, by a typical self-absorbed programmer. David Grossman was a
midlevel IBMer stationed at Cornell University's Theory

Center, a nondescript building hidden away in the southeast corner of the engineering quad. Using a supercomputer connected to an early version of the Internet, Grossman was one of the first people in the world to download the Mosaic browser and experience the graphical world of the Web. Grossman's fecund imagination quickly conjured up a wealth of interesting applications for the nascent technology. But it was an event in February, as snow dusted the ground around the Theory Center, that hardened his determination to help get IBM out in front of what he knew would at the very least be the Next Big Thing—and might very well be the Ultimate Big Thing.

The Winter Olympics had just started in Lillehammer, Norway, and IBM was its official technology sponsor, responsible for collecting and displaying all the results. Watching the games at home, Grossman saw the IBM logo on the bottom of his TV screen and sat through the feel-good ads touting IBM's contribution to the event. But when he sat in front of his UNIX workstation and surfed the Web, he got a totally different picture. A rogue Olympics Web site, run by Sun Microsystems, was taking IBM's raw data feed and presenting it under the Sun banner. "If I didn't know any better," says Grossman, "I would have thought that the data was being provided by Sun. And IBM didn't have a clue as to what was happening on the open Internet. It bothered me."

The fact that IBM's muckety-mucks were clueless about the Web wasn't exactly news to Grossman. When he had landed at IBM a few years earlier, everyone was still using mainframe terminals. "I was shocked," he remembers. "I came from a progressive computing environment and was telling people at IBM that there was this thing called UNIX—there was an Internet. No one knew what I was talking about."

This time, though, he felt embarrassed for IBM, and he was irked. He logged on to the corporate directory and looked up the name of the senior executive in charge of all IBM marketing, Abby Kohnstamm. Then he sent her a message informing her that IBM's Olympic feed

As sober-suited IBM executives scurried through their rounds, Mick Jagger could be heard wailing from the closet.

was being ripped off. A few days later, one of her minions working in Lillehammer called Grossman back. At the end of a frustrating conversation, Grossman had the feeling that one of them was living on another planet. Ever persistent, Grossman tried to send some screen shots from Sun's Web site to IBM's marketing staff in Lillehammer, but IBM's internal e-mail system couldn't cope with the Web software. That didn't stop IBM's diligent legal department from sending Sun a cease-and-desist letter, which succeeded in shutting down the site.

Most frontline employees would have left it at that. But Grossman felt IBM was missing a bigger point: Sun was about to eat Big Blue's lunch. After everyone had come back from the Olympics, he drove down to IBM's headquarters, four hours away in Armonk, New York, to personally show Kohnstamm the Internet.

A Virtual Team Takes Shape

When he arrived, Grossman walked in unattended, a UNIX workstation in his arms. Wearing a programmer's uniform of khakis and an open-necked shirt, he wound his way up to the third floor—the sanctum sanctorum of the largest computer company in the world. Borrowing a T1 line from someone who had been working on a video project, he strung it down the hall to a storage closet where he plugged it into the back of his workstation. He was now ready for his demo—a tour of some early Web sites, including one for the Rolling Stones. As sober-suited IBM executives scurried through their rounds, Mick Jagger could be heard wailing from the closet.

In addition to Kohnstamm, two others were present at that first demo. One was Irving Wladawsky-Berger, head of the supercomputer division where Grossman worked. The other was John Patrick, who sat on a strategy task force with Wladawsky-Berger. Patrick, a career IBMer and lifelong gadget freak, had been head of marketing for the hugely successful ThinkPad laptop computer and was working in corporate strategy, scouting for his next big project. Within minutes, Grossman had his full attention. "When I saw the Web for the first time," says Patrick, "all the bells and whistles went off. Its ability to include colorful, interesting graphics and to link to audio and video content blew my mind."

Not everyone saw what Patrick saw in that primitive first browser. "Two people can see the same thing but have a very different understanding of the implications," he recalls. "A lot of people [would say], 'What's the big deal about the Web?' But I could see that people would do their banking here and get access to all kinds of information. I had been using on-line systems like CompuServe for a long time. For people who weren't already using on-line systems, it was harder for them to see."

Their passions fueled by the Web's limitless possibilities, Patrick and Grossman became IBM's Internet tag team, with Patrick doing the business translation for Grossman and Grossman doing the technology translation for Patrick. Patrick acted as a sponsor and a resource broker. Grossman developed intimate links with the Net-heads in IBM's far-flung development community. "The hardest part for people on the street like me," says Grossman, "was how to get senior-level attention within IBM." Patrick became his mentor and his go-between.

After seeing Grossman's demo, Patrick hired him, and they soon hooked up with another Internet activist within IBM, David Singer. Singer was a researcher in Alameda, California, who had written one of the first Gopher programs, which fetched information off the Net. Grossman and Singer started building a primitive corporate intranet,

Like dissidents using a purloined duplicator in the old Soviet Union, Patrick and Grossman used the Web to build a community of Web fans that would ultimately transform IBM.

and Patrick published a nine-page manifesto extolling the Web. Entitled "Get Connected," the manifesto outlined six ways IBM could leverage the Web:

1. Replace paper communications with e-mail.

2. Give every employee an e-mail address.

3. Make top executives available to customers and investors on-line.

4. Build a home page to better communicate with customers.

5. Print a Web address on everything, and put all marketing on-line.

6. Use the home page for e-commerce.

The Get Connected paper, distributed informally by e-mail, found a ready audience among IBM's unheralded

Internet aficionados. The next step was to set up an on-line news group of the sort that allowed IBM's underground hackers to trade technical tidbits. "Very few people higher up even knew this stuff existed," says Grossman. Within months, more than 300 enthusiasts would join the virtual Get Connected team. Like dissidents using a purloined duplicator in the old Soviet Union, Patrick and Grossman would use the Web to build a community of Web fans that would ultimately transform IBM.

As Patrick's group began to blossom, some argued that he should "go corporate" and turn the nascent Web initiative into an officially sanctioned project. Patrick's boss, senior VP for strategy and development Jim Canavino, disagreed. "You know, we could set up some sort of department and give you a title," Canavino remarked to Patrick, "but I think that would be a bad idea. Try to keep this grassroots thing going as long as possible." Patrick needed to infiltrate IBM rather than manage some splendidly isolated project team. It would be easy for others at IBM to ignore a dinky department, but they couldn't stand in the way of a groundswell.

Still, Canavino wasn't above using his role as head of strategy to give the fledgling initiative a push. To avoid the danger of going quickly from having no IBM Web site to having dozens of uncoordinated ones, Canavino decreed that nobody could build a site without Patrick's approval. Though few in IBM had any inkling of what the Internet would become, Patrick had become IBM's semi-official Internet czar.

"Where's the Buy Button?"

Patrick's volunteer army was a widely dispersed group of Net addicts, many of whom had no idea that others shared their passion. "What John ended up providing,"

says Grossman, "was the ability to articulate and sum-
marize what everyone was doing and to open a lot of
doors." In turn, the Net-heads introduced Patrick to the
culture of the Internet, with its egalitarian ideals and
trial-by-fire approach to developing new technologies.
When the Get Connected conspirators gathered for their
first physical meeting, remembers Grossman, "the question on everybody's lips was, How do we wake this company up?" (For more on this, see "How to Start an Insurrection" at the end of this article.)

Patrick gathered a small group of his Get Connected
renegades, including Grossman, at his vacation house,
set deep in the woods of western Pennsylvania. There
they cobbled together a mock-up of an IBM home page.
The next step was to get through to Gerstner's personal
technology adviser, who agreed to make him available
for a demo of the prospective IBM corporate Web site.
When Gerstner saw the mock-up, his first question was,
"Where's the buy button?" Gerstner wasn't a quick
study—he was an instant study. But Grossman and
Patrick knew that an intrigued CEO wasn't enough.
There were thousands of others who still needed to get
the Internet religion.

Their first chance for a mass conversion came at a
meeting of IBM's top 300 officers on May 11, 1994. Having
schemed to get himself on the agenda, Patrick drove
his point home hard. He started by showing IBM's top
brass some other sites that were already up and running,
including ones done by Hewlett-Packard; Sun Microsystems; the Red Sage restaurant in Washington, D.C.; and
Grossman's six-year-old son Andrew. The point was clear:
on the Web, everyone could have a virtual presence.

Patrick ended the demo by saying, "Oh, by the way,
IBM is going to have a home page too, and this is what it
will look like." He showed the startled executives a

mock-up of www.ibm.com, complete with a 36.2-second
video clip of Gerstner saying, "My name is Lou Gerstner.
Welcome to IBM."

Still, many IBM old-timers remained skeptical. Recalls
Patrick: "A lot of people were saying, 'How do you make
money at this?' I said, 'I have no idea. All I know is that
this is the most powerful, important form of communication both inside and outside the company that has
ever existed.'"

Shortly after the May meeting, Patrick and a few colleagues showed up at one of the first Internet World
trade conventions. The star of the show, with the biggest
booth, was rival Digital Equipment. Like Grossman's
before him, Patrick's competitive fires were stoked. The
next day, the convention's organizers auctioned off space
for the next show, scheduled for December, and Patrick
signed IBM up for the biggest display, at a cost of tens of
thousands of dollars. "It was money I did not have,"
admits Patrick, "but I knew I could find it somehow. If
you don't occasionally exceed your formal authority, you
are not pushing the envelope."

Now that IBM's name was on the line, Patrick had a
rallying point for all of the company's various Internet-
related projects. Here was his chance to seed his message
across the entire company. He sent letters to the general
managers of all the business units asking for anything
they had that smelled like the Internet. They would have
to put in only a little money, he promised, and he would
coordinate everything. It turned out that IBM had a lot
more Web technology brewing than even he had
expected. But none of it was really ready to go to market.
Still, by December, Patrick was able to showcase IBM's
Global Network, as the world's largest Internet service
provider, as well as a Web browser that preceded both

Netscape's Navigator and Microsoft's Internet Explorer. IBM stole the show and became a fixture at every Internet World thereafter.

Constantly fighting IBM's parochialism, Patrick took every opportunity to drive home the point that the Web was a companywide issue and not the preserve of a single division. At the next Internet World, in June 1995, he challenged his compatriots to leave their local biases at the door: "The night before the show, I got everybody together in an auditorium and said, 'We are here because we are the IBM Internet team for the next three days. You are not IBM Austin or IBM Germany.' That is part of the culture of the Internet—boundaryless, flat."

The huge IBM booth generated a lot of curiosity among the show's other participants. When people asked Patrick to whom he reported, he said, "The Internet." When they asked him about his organization, he replied, "You're looking at it, and there are hundreds more."

Throwing Hand Grenades

Patrick was a relentless campaigner, spreading the good word about the Internet in countless speeches inside and outside IBM. "Somebody would invite me to talk about the ThinkPad," he recalls, "and I would come talk about the Internet instead. I'd use the ThinkPad to bring up Web page presentations rather than PowerPoint slides." He also made himself accessible to the media. But even when talking to reporters, his prime constituency was still the vast swath of unconverted IBMers. He just couldn't shut up about the Internet. Says Patrick: "If you believe it, you've got to be out there constantly talking about it, not sometimes, but all the time. If you know you're right, you just keep going."

While Patrick and his crew were throwing Internet
hand grenades into every meeting they could wheedle
their way into, Gerstner was fanning the flames from
above. Gerstner's early belief in the importance of network computing dovetailed nicely with the logic of the
Internet. Having bought into Patrick's pitch, Gerstner
was ever ready to give IBM's Web-heads a boost. He
insisted that the company put its annual and quarterly
reports on the Web, and he signed up to give a keynote
address at Internet World. This was while Bill Gates and
others were still dissing the Web as an insecure medium
for consumer e-commerce. Within IBM, Patrick became
a trusted emissary between the company's buttoned-
down corporate types and the T-shirted buccaneers who
were plugged into Net culture and living on Internet
time. Patrick had the ear of IBM's aristocracy, and his
message was simple and unequivocal: "Miss this and you
miss the future of computing." At the same time, Patrick
convinced Grossman and his ilk that not everyone in the
head office was a Neanderthal. "I used to think that IBM
at senior levels was clueless, that these guys had no idea
how to run a company," says Grossman. "But one of the
many things that has impressed me is that the people
who are running this company are really brilliant businesspeople. Somehow we connected them to the street.
Knowing how to shorten paths to those decision makers
was key."

When IBM finally set up a small, formal Internet
group, with Patrick as chief technical officer, he insisted
that the team stay separate from IBM's traditional software development organization. His logic: "I do believe
there's a benefit in being separate. Otherwise, we'd have
to start going to meetings. Pretty soon we'd be part of
someone else's organization, and a budget cut would
come along, and we'd be gone."

Even with the formal unit in place, Patrick and Grossman didn't disband their grassroots coalition. As the 1996 Summer Olympics approached, the group went through several watershed events. Patrick lent Grossman out for 18 months to corporate marketing, which was in charge of the Olympics project. For the first time, the Olympics would have an official Web site, and IBM would build it. Grossman launched himself into building the site and was soon begging Patrick for extra bodies. "Patrick did the magic to get them hired," says Grossman, "and I morphed from doing the grunt technical work to being Tom Sawyer and getting other people to help whitewash the fence."

To prepare for the Olympics, Grossman and his team had also started developing Web sites for other sporting events such as the 1995 U.S. Open and Wimbledon. For the U.S. Open site, he gave a couple of college interns from MIT the task of writing a program to connect a scoring database to the Web site. "By the end of the summer," remembers Grossman, "we were sitting in a trailer, barely keeping together a Web site with a million people a day pounding away at it for scores. It was held together by Scotch tape, but we were learning about scalability." It was amazing, thought Grossman, that all those people would come to a site merely for sports scores.

IBM's second surprise came in 1996 when a chess match between world champion Garry Kasparov and an IBM supercomputer named Deep Blue generated a flood of global interest. Corporate marketing had asked Grossman earlier to build the Web site for the match, but he was booked with too many other assignments, so the site was outsourced to an advertising agency that did little more than put up a cheesy chessboard. The day of the first match, the site was overloaded with traffic and crashed.

"Nobody had any idea this was going to be such a big deal," says Patrick. IBM went into panic mode. Grossman and a handful of IBM's best Web engineers jumped in to take over the site. With only 36 hours to revamp it before the next match, they got Wladawsky-Berger to pull a $500,000 supercomputer off the assembly line. The site didn't crash again, but the incident raised the anxiety level about the upcoming Olympics. If IBM was having difficulty running a Web site for a chess match, what were the Olympics going to be like? The incident succeeded in convincing a few more skeptics that the Internet was going to be beyond Big.

The Olympics site had to be able to withstand anything. Patrick went tin-cupping again, asking all the general managers to lend him their best people and best equipment. He got not one supercomputer, but three, and his team grew to about 100 people. By the time it was over, IBM had built what was then the world's largest Web site, which withstood up to 17 million hits a day with few shutdowns. The content on the site was replicated on servers across four continents. IBM even learned how to do a little e-commerce when a demo site for on-line ticket sales attracted a flood of credit card numbers and $5 million in orders.

The Power of Results

For Patrick and Grossman, the Olympics was just one more high-profile way to show IBM the possibilities of the Internet. It was also an easy way to get funding for development. "I used the Olympics as a front," admits Grossman. "What I was doing, without telling anyone, was getting computing resources. I also thought the fastest way to get IBM to change was to work from the outside in. If IBM saw itself written about in the papers, then it would change faster than if we got mired in an internal process."

Grossman's on-the-fly development, in public no less, was the complete antithesis of IBM's traditional way of doing things, which was to push developers to perfect products before letting them out the door. It was the difference between improv comedy and a carefully rehearsed Broadway play. The old model didn't make much sense on the Web, where if something breaks, you can fix it without sending out millions of CD-ROMs with new software. You just change the software on the server, and everyone who logs on automatically gets the new version.

Grossman and Patrick quickly concluded that creating Web-enabled software called for a new set of software development principles, which they summarized and shared within the burgeoning IBM Web community:

- Start simple; grow fast.

- Trial by fire.

- Just don't inhale (the stale air of orthodoxy).

- Just enough is good enough.

- Skip the krill (go to the top of the food chain when you're trying to sell your idea).

- Wherever you go, there you are (the Net has no bounds).

- No blinders.

- Take risks; make mistakes quickly; fix them fast.

- Don't get pinned down (to any one way of thinking).

Much of the technology that Grossman and his crew first prototyped would later make its way into industrial-strength products. For instance, the Web server software developed for the Olympics evolved into a product called Websphere, and much of what Grossman's group learned formed the basis for a Web-hosting business that today supports tens of thousands of Web sites.

Following the Olympics, the Internet group stepped up its proselytizing within IBM. Grossman, who had become the senior technical staff member on Patrick's team, set up an Internet lab to bring in executives from all over the company to experience the Web's possibilities. Patrick's group also started a project called "Web Ahead," which worked to revolutionize the company's own IT systems through Internet technology. For instance, the team took the old terminal-based corporate directory and wrote a Java application that gave it a great graphical interface and cool features. With a few clicks, employees could look up a colleague, see what computer skills he or she had, and then ask the directory to list every other employee at IBM with those same skills. These "Blue Pages" were an instant hit.

"We have never been a threat to any other part of the company. From the beginning, our goal was to help IBM become the Internet Business Machines company."

Only a few dozen people officially worked for the Internet group, so Patrick was constantly pleading to borrow people (who were usually already part of his virtual team) from other departments. In this effort, his most important ally was the team's ever-lengthening list of success stories. People could argue with position papers, but they couldn't argue with results. "I have never been turned down on anything I have asked for, and I have asked for a lot," he says. "I would go to a general manager and say, 'I need you to pull some disk drives from the assembly line, and I need your top engineer. What you will get out of it is unique. Your guy is going to come back to your group, and you are going to have a hell of a reference story to talk about. It will be great PR. We will make your stuff work on the Internet.'" Patrick had gained credibility without a big job title or a megabudget.

Patrick was hard to refuse, partly because it was clear that he was operating in IBM's interests as a whole and not just fighting for his own little group. As he puts it, "I didn't have any allegiance to any one product group. Although I had a budget that came out of the software group, I didn't think of us as part of the software group. When somebody called us and asked for help, we didn't ask them for a budget code. We'd say, 'Sure.' We have never been a threat to any other part of the company. From the beginning, our goal was to help IBM become the Internet Business Machines company."

Patrick was quick to assure would-be donors that the relationships he was forging worked both ways. He would borrow people from various business units, but at any given time, about a quarter of his own people would be out on loan to other units, and Web Ahead alumni were regularly posted to permanent positions across IBM. When that happened, he would tell his remaining staff, "We did not lose Bill. We colonized the network hardware division. Now there is one of us living there."

Again and again, throughout their Internet campaign, Patrick and Grossman broke long-standing IBM rules and overstepped the boundaries of their own authority. But because their cause was so important and their commitment to IBM's success so visibly selfless, they got away with things that had often sunk careers at Big Blue. Then and now, Patrick is unapologetic: "If you think of yourself as being in a box with boundaries, you're not going to have any breakthroughs. If [people on my team] come to me and say, 'We failed because we didn't have the authority to do something,' I'll say that's crazy."

Inside IBM and out, Patrick and Grossman are today recognized for their pivotal contribution to their company's e-business metamorphosis. With the support of a prochange CEO, these two unlikely heroes—a software nerd and a corporate staffer—helped IBM do something it hadn't done for a couple of decades: lead from the front.

How to Start an Insurrection

Is it clear to you that your company needs to be shaken up? Then it's time you became a revolutionary. Here are seven steps for organizing a corporate insurrection.

1. **Establish a point of view.** In a world of people who stand for nothing more than more of the same, a sharply articulated POV is your greatest asset. It's a sword that lets you slay the dragons of precedent. It's a rudder that lets you steer a steady course when others are blown about by fad and whim. And it's a beacon that attracts those who are looking for something worthy of their allegiance. A powerful POV is credible, coherent, compelling, and commercial. To be credible, it must be founded on unimpeachable data. To be coherent, it must be logical, laying out a bulletproof argument. To be compelling, it must

speak to people's emotions, telling them why your cause will make a difference in the world. To be commercial, it must have a clear link to the bottom line.

2. **Write a manifesto.** It's not enough to have an ideology; you have to be able to pass it on, to infect others with your ideas. Like Thomas Paine, whose *Common Sense* became the inspiration for the American Revolution, you have to write a manifesto. It doesn't have to be long, but it must capture people's imaginations. It must paint a picture of what is and what is coming that causes discomfort. And it must provide a vision of what could be that inspires hope.

3. **Create a coalition.** You can't change the direction of your company all by yourself. You need to build a coalition, a group of colleagues who share your vision and passion. It's easy to dismiss corporate rebels when they are fragmented and isolated. But when they present themselves as a coordinated group, speaking in a single voice, they cannot be ignored. And remember, as you struggle to attract recruits to your cause, you will have an advantage over top management. Your army will be made up of volunteers; theirs will be composed of conscripts. Conscripts fight to stay alive; volunteers fight to win.

4. **Pick your targets.** Sooner or later, a manifesto has to become a mandate if it's going to make a difference. The movement has to get the blessing of the suits. That's why activists always identify and target a potential champion—someone or a group of someones that can yank the real levers of power. Ultimately, the support of senior management is the object of your crusade. Make an effort to understand them—the pressures they face, the objectives they have to fulfill. Find some

who are searching for help and ideas, and go after them. If necessary, bend your ideals a bit to fit their goals. And don't forget that leaders are often more receptive to new thinking than are the minions who serve them.

5. **Co-opt and neutralize.** Some activists further their causes by confronting and embarrassing their adversaries. Such tactics may work in the public sphere, but in a business setting they'll probably get you fired. You need to disarm and co-opt, not demean and humiliate. To win over IBM's feudal lords, John Patrick constructed a set of win-win propositions for them: Lend me some talent, and I'll build a showcase for your products. Let me borrow a few of your top people, and I'll send them back with prototypes of cool new products. Reciprocity wins converts; ranting leaves you isolated and powerless.

6. **Find a translator.** Imagine how a buttoned-down dad looks at a daughter who comes home with green hair and an eyebrow ring. That's the way top management is likely to view you and your coconspirators. And that's why you need a translator, someone who can build a bridge between you and the people with the power. At IBM, Patrick was a translator for Dave Grossman. He helped the top brass understand the connection between the apparent chaos of the Web and the disciplined world of large-scale corporate computing. Senior staffers and newly appointed executives are often good translator candidates—they're usually hungry for an agenda to call their own.

7. **Win small, win early, win often.** None of your organizing efforts is worth anything if you can't demonstrate that your ideas actually work. You need results. Start small. Unless you harbor kamikaze instincts, search for demon-

stration projects that won't sink you or your cause if they should fail—for some of them will fail. You may have to put together a string of successful projects before top management starts throwing money your way. You have to help your company feel its way toward revolutionary opportunities, step by step. And as your record of wins gets longer, you'll find it much easier to make the transition from an isolated initiative to an integral part of the business. Not only will you have won the battles, you will have won the war.

Originally published in July–August 2000
Reprint R00406

The author acknowledges the assistance of Erick Schonfeld in the preparation of this article.

About the Contributors

MICHAEL BEER is Cahners-Rabb Professor of Business Administration at Harvard Business School, where he teaches in the areas of organization effectiveness, human resource management, and organizational change. Prior to joining the Harvard faculty, he was Director of Organization Research and Development at Corning, Inc., where he was responsible for stimulating a number of innovations in management. He has authored or coauthored several books and many articles. *The Critical Path to Corporate Renewal*, which deals with the problem of large-scale corporate change, won the Johnson, Smith, and Knisley Award for the best book on executive leadership in 1991 and was a finalist for the Academy of Management Book Award that year. In the last several years, he has developed and researched a process by which top teams can manage strategic change in a way that integrates their business and and organizational capability building objectives as advocated in the article he coauthored for this volume. He is Cofounder and Chairman of the Center for Organizational Fitness, which works with top teams who want to learn how to manage such a change process. Professor Beer has served on the editorial board of several journals and the board of governors of the Academy of Management, and has consulted with many *Fortune* 500 companies. His most recent book, *Breaking the Code of Change*, deals with many of the issues raised in the article, "Cracking the Code of Change," included in this volume.

JIM COLLINS is the coauthor of *Built to Last: Successful Habits of Visionary Companies* and the author *of Good to Great: Why Some Companies Make the Leap . . . And Others Don't.* He operates a management research and teaching laboratory in Boulder, Colorado.

LINDA GIOJA has consulted with CEOs and executives at such companies as Allstate, Sears, and Hughes Space and Communications. She now leads dialogues in national policy forums at the Aspen Institute and for the California Environmental Dialogue, a group of more than twenty-five energy companies, automakers, high-tech companies, and government and environmental organizations working on the state's environmental policy. She lives in Austin, Texas.

GARY HAMEL is Founder and Chairman of Strategos, a company dedicated to helping its clients develop revolutionary strategies. He is also Visiting Professor of Strategic and International Management at London Business School. Hamel has led initiatives within many of the world's leading companies. In his work he helps companies first to imagine and then to create the new rules, new businesses, and new industries that will define the industrial landscape of the future. He has published numerous articles in the *Harvard Business Review, Fortune, Sloan Management Review,* and *The Wall Street Journal* and has introduced such breakthrough concepts as strategic intent, core competence, corporate imagination, expeditionary marketing, and strategy as stretch. His book, *Competing for the Future,* with C.K. Prahalad has been hailed by many journals as one of the decade's most influential business books, and by *Business Week* as "Best Management Book of the Year." His most recent book, *Leading the Revolution,* was published in September 2000 and was Amazon.com's pick as Business Book of the Year.

HOLLIS HEIMBOUCH is the Editorial Director at Harvard Business School Press and a contributing editor to the *Harvard Business Review.*

JON MELIONES is Professor of Pediatrics and Anesthesia at Duke University Medical Center, Chief of Critical Care, and the former Chief Medical Director for the Duke Children's Hospital. He is board certified in Pediatrics, Pediatric Cardiology, and Pediatric Critical Care Medicine. As Chief Executive of PracticingSmarter Inc., an organization credited with providing proven enterprise-wide performance management solutions for the healthcare industry, Dr. Meliones is responsible for setting the vision and direction of the company and establishing the clinical foundation for its performance management products and services. He has served on the boards of various academic journals and medical societies and has held leadership positions for these, including President and Senior Editor. In addition to numerous awards for accomplishment in the academic arena, Dr. Meliones has received and continues to receive recognition for his creativity, innovation, and performance results in personalizing and applying the balanced scorecard to healthcare management. He is recognized by Dr. Robert Kaplan, Balanced Scorecard Cofounder with Dr. David Norton, as an industry leader and the only proven implementer of the balanced scorecard in the healthcare industry.

MARK MILLEMANN, now an independent consultant, was a senior advisor to CSC Index. He lives in Portland, Oregon.

NITIN NOHRIA is the Richard P. Chapman Professor of Business Administration and Chairman of the Organizational Behavior Unit at the Harvard Business School. His research interests center on leadership and organizational change. His

latest book, The *Arc of Ambition*, coauthored with Jim
Champy, examines the role of ambition in the making (and
breaking) of great achievers. He is currently working on a
book entitled *Changing Fortunes*, which examines how this
vibrant economic sector came to be called the "old economy"
and what its future prospects are. Professor Nohria has written several other critically acclaimed books including, *Breaking the Code of Change, Fast Forward, Beyond the Hype, Building the Information Organization*, and *The Differentiated
Network*, which won the 1998 George R. Terry Award. Professor Nohria lectures to corporate audiences around the globe
and serves on the advisory boards of several firms. He has
been interviewed by ABC, CNN, and NPR, and cited frequently
in *Business Week, The Economist, Financial Times, Fortune,
New York Times*, and *The Wall Street Journal*.

At the time this article was originally published, BILL PAR-
CELLS was Director of Football Operations for the New York
Jets. He has served as head coach of three professional football teams: the New York Giants (1983–1990), the New England Patriots (1993–1997), and the Jets (1997–1999).

RICHARD PASCALE is a writer, a leading business consultant worldwide, and an associate fellow of Templeton College, Oxford University, England. He is the coauthor (with
Mark Millemann and Linda Gioja) of *Surfing the Edge of
Chaos*. Dr. Pascale also authored the 1990 book, *Managing
on the Edge*, and coauthored the 1981 best-selling book, *The
Art of Japanese Management*, with Anthony Athos. He was
on the faculty of Stanford Business School for twenty years,
and has written numerous articles for leading business management publications.

RICH TEERLINK retired as Chairman and CEO of Harley-
Davidson in 1999. During his eighteen years with Harley, he

served as Chief Financial Officer, President, Chief Executive Officer, and Chairman of the Board. He was appointed to the board of directors in 1982 and was part of the leadership team that led the revitalization of the company. In 1986, he helped to guide Harley back to public ownership. Prior to joining Harley, he had the benefit of working at large and small, public and private companies at both the corporate and divisional levels in line and staff assignments. During that time he held key executive positions with Herman Miller, RTE Corporation, Union Special Corporation, and MGD Graphic Systems. He currently serves on the boards of directors of Harley-Davidson, Johnson Controls, Snap-on Incorporated, and Bering Truck Corporation. Mr. Teerlink is a frequent speaker to business organizations internationally and an active participant in many business and community organizations.

Index